MW00723971

THE CIVIL WAR IN OXFORDSHIRE

DAVID EDDERSHAW

WITH A CONTRIBUTION BY ELEANOR ROBERTS

ALAN SUTTON PUBLISHING LIMITED

XFORDSHIRE BOOKS

First published in 1995
Alan Sutton Publishing Limited · Phoenix Mill · Far Thrupp
Stroud · Gloucestershire

Oxfordshire Books · Oxfordshire County Council · Leisure and Arts
Central Library · Westgate · Oxford

British Library Cataloguing in Publication Data

Eddershaw, David
Civil War in Oxfordshire
I. Title II. Roberts, Eleanor
942.57062

ISBN 0-7509-0600-6

Cover illustration: The Siege of Oxford *by Jan de Wyck, 1689 (in the
collection of the Earl of Dartmouth presently on loan to the Museum of Oxford)*

Typeset in 11/14 Bembo.
Typesetting and origination by
Alan Sutton Publishing Limited.
Printed in Great Britain by
Ebenezer Baylis, Worcester.

CONTENTS

ACKNOWLEDGEMENTS

My thanks are due firstly to Eleanor Roberts for her major contribution to this book. Her knowledge and expertise as archivist for the records of the Oxford City Council have brought to light important material on the role of the city government during the Royalist occupation, described in Chapter 4.

I should like to thank the following institutions for permission to quote from documents in their collections: the Bodleian Library; the Centre for Oxfordshire Studies; Oxfordshire Archives; Oxford City Council; Exeter College, Oxford. Extracts from the diary of Bulstrode Whitelock are reproduced by permission of the British Academy from Ruth Spalding (ed.), *Records of Social and Economic History, New Series XII, The Diary of Bulstrode Whitelock 1605–1675*, 1990. Extracts from J. Washbourn (ed.), *Bibliotheca Gloucestrensis*, 1825, are taken from the copy in the Hyett Collection at Gloucestershire Record Office.

Illustrations are reproduced on the following pages by kind permission of: Ashmolean Museum, Oxford, 'The Souldiers in their passage to York' (CI370): 162; the Bodleian Library, Oxford, Christ Church from *Oxonia Illustrata* by David Loggan, 1675 (Plate 27, Arch. Antiq. All. 13): 4; the Syndics of Cambridge University Library: 117; Centre for Oxfordshire Studies: 3, 23, 28, 34, 36, 91, 158; Paul Fisher: xii; the owner, from family archives deposited in the Gloucestershire Record Office (ref. D1245 FF76): 83; in the collection of the Earl of Dartmouth presently on loan to the Museum of Oxford: 138; the National Portrait Gallery, London: 14, 31, 100; Oxford City Council: 54, 55, 57 (photograph: Courtauld Institute of Art), 63; Oxfordshire Archives: 16, 126.

INTRODUCTION: MEMORIES OF WAR

On Thursday 10 May 1660 Charles II, newly restored to the throne of England after the death of Oliver Cromwell and the collapse of his Commonwealth, was proclaimed in the streets of Oxford. The newsheet *Mercurius Publicus* described the scene:

> The Mayor, with the Mace bearer the Serjeants and other Officers riding before him, rode in his scarlet and formalities, with the Recorder, the Aldermen, Bayliffs and others in scarlet, and about a hundred of the Council in their gowns . . . proceeded to the Conduit and there the King was proclaimed . . . At the end of every proclamation the . . . shouting from a very great concourse of people, and volleys of shot from the souldiers, made the very ayr to rebound with ecchoes of joy; the Conduit ran Claret at two places about three houres, a thing never done here before, and many hundred bottles of wine disposed of by the Mayor and the Council to the Spectators; and also divers barrels of beer that was set in the streets common for any body, and a hundred dozens of bread that was disposed to the poor.
>   . . . The whole business was managed with such general and cordial manifestations of joy, that did clearly evidence that old and unfained loyalty, that the generality of this City have ever born to His Majesties Father, our late King of most glorious memory, which they have done and do bear to our Royal Soveraign King Charles the Second whom God preserve.

There is a very great contrast between this picture and the somewhat nervous welcome given to Charles I by the City Council when he took possession of Oxford after the battle of Edgehill in 1642.

Above all, the reference to 'that old and unfained loyalty' which the people of Oxford are said to have shown towards Charles I, could hardly have been further from the truth. Many of them, led by those members of the City Council who had not left Oxford to join the supporters of Parliament, had spent the entire period of the war obstructing his wishes as much as they dared and showing great reluctance in complying with his commands.

It is not difficult to see why men like the author of *Mercurius Publicus*, who welcomed the restoration of the monarchy in 1660, would be keen to emphasize the degree of public support, and those who had opposed the restored king's father would not want to draw attention to the fact at that time. It is also undoubtedly true that many people who had originally fought for Cromwell had become disillusioned with his Commonwealth and willingly accepted the return of Charles II. Perhaps there was an understandable desire to return to the good old days before the war and to soften the memory of the more immediate past. Even if the history of the Civil War could not be completely rewritten, at least the picture could be repainted so that much of the horror, suffering, bitterness and strength of feeling about the issues (especially uncomfortable arguments about democracy) faded into the background. This natural tendency, together with the passage of time, has resulted in a rather vague impression of such an important but horrific episode in our history being left in the minds of many people today.

Three hundred and fifty years later the popular image of the Civil War is often a misleading one of merry Cavaliers in plumed hats galloping about the countryside pursuing long-faced Roundheads (in tall black hats), with as little concern for reality as most people feel about cowboys and Indians in an old Western. Re-enactment societies take themselves very seriously, assiduously researching details of costume, weapons, armour, tactics and the lives of seventeenth-century soldiers generally, so that they present to their spectators and to themselves an illusion of authenticity, but the very circumstances of their performances – as Sunday afternoon entertainment – and the obvious reluctance, and indeed impossibility, of portraying the real horror and violence of war, only serve to perpetuate the myth.

This region has its share of local traditions derived from the Civil War, often attached to places which played a part in it. Not surprisingly, tales

Watching a re-enactment of the first battle of Newbury.

of ghostly armies refighting the battle of Edgehill were common in that area soon after the event and are still remembered today, perhaps because the horror of that first terrible encounter and the 1,500 dead impressed itself so forcibly on the minds of local people that for a long time afterwards they suffered the terrifyingly real nightmares and hallucinations that are a symptom of shock in any age. Individual and very personal suffering is recorded in the legend in Wallingford, which recounts that the daughter of one of the town's landlords fell in love with a sergeant in the king's army, but when he was killed in a soldiers' brawl in the pub she shut herself away in an upstairs room, mixing her tears with soot from the chimney and painting black tear-drops on the walls. There was a King's Room in Shiel Farm, Alvescot (now demolished), in which Charles is said to have stayed before Edgehill and again before Newbury. Both occasions seem improbable as the farm did not lie near the routes he was likely to be taking to either place, but few of the many similar stories can be proved or disproved. The association of the king with the Royalist Hotel in Stow-on-the-Wold and of Cromwell with Cromwell Cottage, Marston, where the siege of Oxford was coordinated,

The 'Tear-drop Room' at the George Hotel, Wallingford,
said to have been decorated by the heartbroken daughter
of the landlord, who mixed her tears with soot from the
chimney and painted tear-drops on the wall when her
Royalist soldier sweetheart was killed in a pub brawl.

are more authentic, but no such claim can surely be made for the
curiously named Cromwell Business Park in Chipping Norton. Henley
boasts Rupert's Elm, from which he hanged a spy, and Oxford has North
Parade and South Parade, said to mark the front lines of the defenders
and besiegers of the city respectively (hence North Parade is further
south than South Parade).

The Royalist Hotel, Stow-on-the-Wold. This is one of a number of
buildings which claim association with Charles I.

It was not only in Ireland that Oliver Cromwell was used as a
bogeyman to frighten children centuries after his armies used such
cruelty against the garrisons of Drogheda and Wexford. Flora
Thompson writing about her Oxfordshire childhood in the 1880s
recalls that the older generation of mothers in the tiny hamlet of
Juniper Hill, used the threat of 'old Crummell' to restrain disobedient
children. Clearly the fear of his soldiers still lingered in folk memory in
that north-eastern corner of the county.

There are surprisingly few physical remains to remind modern
generations about the war, even some of the most substantial having
long since disappeared. It is almost impossible on the ground to find
any evidence for the extensive earthworks erected around the city of
Oxford. Apart from a section of earth mound in the garden of
Wadham College, only old maps, de Wyck's painting in the Museum
of Oxford and some recent archaeological excavation show where
these elaborate defences were laboriously constructed by soldiers,
students and the often unwilling citizens of Oxford to the design of a
Dutch military engineer, their progress anxiously inspected by the

Only the portcullis symbol over the arched entrance to
Banbury's Castle Shopping Centre remains to remind
today's shoppers of the dreadful suffering of the
townspeople who endured two long sieges of the castle
during the Civil War.

king. The inhabitants of Banbury today have only the name of their
Castle Shopping Centre to remind them of the castle itself, which
played such a vital strategic role in the war and was at the centre of a
siege which left half their town in ruins. In the 1930s a handful of
silver coins was discovered in an old barn at Wolvercote where they
had remained hidden since 1646, but by whom and in what precise
circumstances we can only guess. As well as normal coins they
included a shilling minted in Oxford from silver confiscated from the

colleges. A Civil War sword was found thrust into the thatch of a cottage in Chadlington, but again one can only guess at the details of the story that such objects tell.

By their nature wars destroy more than they create, and it is often the absence of a building or damage to one that remains that is the record of this civil war. Abingdon, Wantage and Burford no longer have their medieval crosses, and numerous churches claim to have suffered damage to monuments and statues at the hands of zealous puritan soldiers. The lopsided appearance of St James' Church, Radley, is due to the destruction of the north aisle and one side of the nave when Parliament troops attacked some Royalists who had fortified it. Ducklington's unusual medieval stone carvings depicting the life of the Virgin have been mutilated, perhaps by Waller's troops when they occupied the village in 1644, for whom they would have been an obvious target. (But they could equally well have been damaged by the early Protestants at the time of the Reformation, a century earlier.)

Very few of the many soldiers who died in Oxfordshire have left any memorial by which they, and the cause for which they gave their lives, might be remembered by today's inhabitants. High-ranking officers and courtiers earned inscriptions in Christ Church Cathedral and the deaths of the Parliamentarian John Hampden and the Royalist Viscount Falkland are both commemorated by memorials elsewhere which were erected in the nineteenth century, but of the junior officers and common soldiers only the names of the Leveller victims are recorded on plaques – erected even more recently in Burford and Oxford. Many more were buried anonymously, sometimes with a pitifully brief entry in the register of some parish where the locals knew nothing of them. These are typical entries, both from Deddington: 'Dec 1st, a souldier, a Frenchmen, who died in our field'; 'Dec 25th a poor souldier'.

A diligent search among burial registers will also reveal the names of hundreds of civilians as well as soldiers who died in the plague- and typhus-ridden war years, but their deaths are overshadowed in popular memory by those of the Great Plague of London, just twenty years later. In some parishes the absence of any registers or a gap covering this period speaks eloquently of the breakdown of local administration. In the Hanwell register is a note that it was 'lost in the late wares 1642–1649, when it was found in Oxforde'. None of these things is obvious, however, to any but historians. Other people may see the heartfelt words inscribed in this century on the bridge at Cropredy, scene of the county's fiercest battle, which speaks for all those who suffered: 'From Civil War Good Lord Deliver Us.'

The events are only one aspect of the war. Even more important, but perhaps harder to remember, are the causes of such an outbreak. A conscious attempt has been made in recent years, by adherents of the political left, to keep alive the memory of the Levellers, and to use the annual commemoration at Burford to raise issues of democracy which still have relevance today. During the debate on the election of a new Speaker of the House of Commons in 1992, allusion was made not only to the well-known words of Speaker Lenthal (an Oxfordshire man) in the Long Parliament, but one historically aware MP asserted that the divine right of kings was 'alive and well in the person of the Prime Minister', referring to what he saw as the lack of real accountability to the people except at general elections. Although the

Levellers' Day celebrations in Burford, 1994.

circumstances of the seventeenth century are clearly very different from those of the twentieth, it is the continuing relevance of some of the underlying issues that makes the Civil War so interesting today, and so important to remember.

Although none of the most important battles took place in this county (Chalgrove was no more than a quick skirmish and even Cropredy Bridge does not compare in scale or significance with Marston Moor or Naseby), Oxfordshire was at the very centre of the war from the moment the king occupied it and made Oxford his military and administrative headquarters until he left it to surrender to the Scottish army in 1646. Three years later it was again in Oxfordshire that the final stages in the Leveller affair were played out, indicating the limits of democracy for the new regime. It used to be thought that life continued much as usual away from the scene of the main fighting, but although the oral and a good deal of the written evidence has been lost in the intervening centuries, our own experience of war and what clues do still survive make it clear that this could not have been true, and certainly not in the city and county of Oxford.

In the context of this book the term 'Oxfordshire' has been used fairly loosely to describe a region with Oxford at its centre. In a war strategic considerations are more important than administrative boundaries. It is, of course, an anachronism to write in terms of the modern county boundaries, which since 1974 have made the Vale of White Horse part of Oxfordshire, whereas at the time of the Civil War this was clearly Berkshire, with Abingdon as its county town. Wallingford, being on the other side of the Thames, was also in that county, but both places were so important to the fate of the Royalist headquarters at Oxford that it is sensible to include them in this account. There will occasionally be reference to places beyond even the modern county, such as Edgehill or Donnington Castle near Newbury, because they, too, have direct strategic links with Oxford. Events in the rest of the country, including all the major battles, will only be mentioned to set the Oxfordshire experience in its context.

The authors hope that this account of events in Oxfordshire will help people today to realize the important part played by this county, and to appreciate something of the excitement, hardship, suffering

and ideals of its inhabitants at that time. It does not claim to be a
scholarly work; with a few exceptions most of the sources are already
well known and extensive use has been made of the work of other
historians. Our aim is simply to bring all this together into a realistic
account of the Civil War so that local people going about their daily
lives in Oxfordshire, or visitors to the county, may be prompted to
pause occasionally in some familiar modern surrounding and recollect
the fierceness and intensity of the struggles that happened there more
than 350 years ago.

CHAPTER 1

SEVENTEENTH-CENTURY OXFORDSHIRE

> The aire mild, temperate and delicate; the land fertile, pleasant and bounteous; in a word both Heaven and Earth accord to make the inhabitants healthful and happy.

Although this description of Oxfordshire by William Camden in his *Britannia*, first published in 1586, may be a bit over the top, it does convey the county's reputation at that time, and in the seventeenth century, as one of the most favoured parts of the kingdom. Its pleasant villages and manor-houses nestled in a productive landscape, served by prosperous market towns with the city of Oxford and its already ancient university at the centre – and all this within convenient reach of the capital. There were certainly close links with London in the first half of the seventeenth century as there are today, and regular movement of both people and goods by road and river. There had been problems with river transport on the Thames for many years because of the conflicting interests of millers (who wished to restrict the flow of water downstream by building weirs) and the transporters of goods. The Thames Commissioners, even though empowered by an Act of Parliament in 1606 to make the river navigable, were so despairing of getting the necessary works done, that in 1611 they allowed a load of timber intended for this work to be sold off to Sir Thomas Bodley for his new library. Improvements were finally made, however, locks being constructed at Iffley and Sandford, and the first barge from London arrived in Oxford in 1635. The new pound locks were called 'turnpikes' and tolls were levied on barges passing through them. Bulky goods like building stone and malt, which had always been important local 'exports' could now be moved much more easily, contributing to the prosperity of local businessmen. At the same time restrictions were placed on the heaviest vehicles using the Oxford to London road in the hope of protecting its unmetalled surface from further damage. Waggons pulled by teams of five or more horses were banned in 1630, although for a time Archbishop Laud, as Chancellor of the University, obtained a special exemption for university carriers.

In spite of the apparent difficulties, however, private travel between Oxford and London could be surprisingly quick. Bulstrode Whitelock, a prosperous parliamentary lawyer and owner of Phyllis Court at Henley, described with fatherly pride how his daughter Frances 'being butt 12 years old, rode in a day singly on horse backe from Phillis Court to London', and he himself made the return journey after attending the House and reached home by the evening. Only two days before he had made a combined road and river journey leaving Phyllis Court early and 'coming into the House before they rose'. A more leisurely way of travelling upstream (and more expensive because of the tolls and boat hire) back to Oxford was to go the whole way by boat, but this took twice as long: 'Whitelocke and his wife and children and Mr Hall and his wife and their servants took three payre of oares to go by water from London to Phillis Court. They dined at Hampton Court and came by 8 att night to Windsor and lodged there. . . . The next day they came to Phillis Court: this way by water is the most easy and pleasant but the most chargeable way of traveyle.'

Even more important people than Bulstrode Whitelock made this journey. Both James I and Charles I knew Oxfordshire well, long before Charles chose to make Oxford his wartime capital. Both stayed sometimes at their royal manor of Woodstock, where the old palace was described by a traveller in 1634 as 'ancient, large, strong and magnificent, so it was sweet, delightful and sumptuous, and sytuated on a fayre hill'. Among other features he noted 'a counsell chamber, curiously archt, and a neat chappell near it where our Queene heard Masse; and divers other fayre and large rooms for the nobilitie and officers of the court.' A rather less flattering opinion had been expressed by Sir Robert Cecil, who stayed there as a member of the court of James I and complained that he found it overcrowded, damp and unsavoury 'for there was no savour but of the cows and pigs'. Some of the court who could not be accommodated in the palace had

The old royal palace of Woodstock.

to lodge in tents in the grounds or at the inns of the town, which had always profited from such trade. In August 1638 Thomas Wyatt, the rector of the small parish of Ducklington, recorded in his journal that King Charles was staying at Woodstock and had killed a stag not far from Ducklington, and then on 31 August that he actually came through Ducklington. One can imagine the excitement in the village.

Archbishop Laud entertained Charles I on his official visit to the university in 1636 in an extremely lavish style, of which contemporary accounts survive. Laud's own college was St John's, where he had just provided a new library but the king lodged at Christ Church because of its greater size. The climax of the visit, however, was a vast banquet at St John's which one witness called

A mightye feast, equall to any I have heard of . . . I doe wonder where there cold be found mouthes to eate it, for without consideration of presents, his Grace had provided suffitient to feede, nay feast, all from the highest ranke of men, even to the guard and footmen of both courts. His presents were immense . . . Your kinsman sent a huge fatt oxe, 20 fatt sheepe, a brace of stags and a brace of buckes, the Earl of Bristow 20 fatt sheepe, 20 brace of fesants, My Ld Tom Sommersett a huge fatt ox, besides fowle and extraordinary fishe, Dr. Stewart Clarke of the Closett and Dean of Chichester 20 dozen of partridges, Sir Thos. Mownson such a present of foule as Pay, the clerke of the kitchen, told me he never sawe presented to a prince by any subject, but the Bishop of Winchester exeeded all for venison, fish and foule . . .

The cost of this stupendous banquet and the play which followed it was given as £2,666 1s 7d, which in terms of the seventeenth century represented a vast sum of money. In the light of such splendid accommodation, lavish demonstrations of loyalty and such generous hospitality, it is no surprise that the king chose Oxford as his capital when London turned against him.

The roads of Oxfordshire were busy with other travellers to whom such amounts were unimaginable: packmen, pedlars, tinkers and higglers plied their wares from village to village while local people took cows, sheep, pigs and geese to market and drovers herded larger numbers of the same livestock towards more distant destinations along

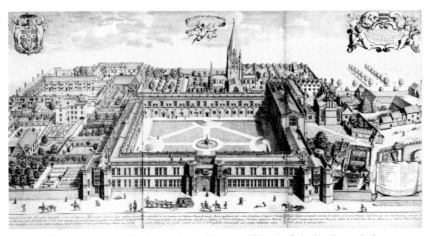

Christ Church, Oxford, was the residence of Charles I during its period as the Royalist capital.

well-trodden routes. For all of them unimpeded travel along the local road network was important, but would be one of the first casualties of the war. There were also numbers of unemployed destitute people travelling about in search of work or simply the next meal or place to sleep. Liable to be whipped or at best moved on to the next parish, perhaps the war would give them a chance of employment in one of the armies.

The prosperity of towns like Banbury, Thame, Wantage, Chipping Norton, Watlington, and a dozen others like them, depended on their markets and fairs. In the larger places there could be more than one market-day each week, perhaps specializing in different kinds of produce or livestock, and several fairs throughout the year, each one perhaps lasting several days and centered around the feast of a locally celebrated saint. Abingdon had as many as seven annual fairs throughout the year in the 1620s. Banbury already had an important livestock market which gave names to streets like Beast Market, Hog Market, Horsefair and Corn Market. A traveller in 1622 described Bicester as 'a very good market for all manner of cattle and well supplied with all kinds of trades', and the evidence in wills and inventories of the period shows what a range of trades would grow up around a flourishing market: tanners, glovers, saddlers, clothiers, weavers, fullers and maltsters all worked in Bicester. In Thame there were brickmakers as well as the usual trades, and everywhere there were blacksmiths, wheelwrights and carpenters. Oxford boasted nearly a hundred trades serving the extravagant demands of the university as well as the needs of local people. Control of Oxford's market, however, was one of many points of contention in the fierce rivalry between city and university going back to the notorious St Scholastica's day riot nearly three hundred years earlier. A new market charter in 1636 confirmed the university's right to collect the tolls, and sparked off another round of disputes. A few years later the traders themselves tried to form an irregular combination to forestall the market by meeting carriers and others bringing produce from the surrounding countryside outside the town, buying from them there and then reselling at inflated prices in the market.

Some of the leading merchants and tradesmen became wealthy and influential men in the city, with a place among 'The Thirteen', as the

City Council was known. Similar ambitions were evident in other towns among successful businessmen. In 1607 the wealthier burgesses of Chipping Norton obtained a royal charter from James I incorporating the town as a borough with fourteen of their own number forming the governing body, their dignity sustained by all sorts of pomp and ceremony and the fees they could charge for allowing others to practise a trade in the borough. The tradesmen of Bicester were unusual in never seeking borough status and claimed that they were better off without it, whereas those of Burford, who had for centuries assumed the status of an independent corporation without having received an official grant, received instead a nasty shock to their pride and their pockets when the new lord of the manor, Judge Lawrence Tanfield, succesfully challenged them and reclaimed his rights as lord.

The wealth of successful businessmen was sometimes used in charitable works like the founding of schools and almshouses. In the first half of the century Robert Vesey, a wool merchant, founded a free grammar school at Bampton with a bequest of £300 and the very

Almshouses in Chipping Norton, endowed in 1646 by Henry Cornish, a leading citizen of the town and Puritan sympathizer.

attractive range of almshouses for 'eight poor widows of Godly conversation' were endowed at Chipping Norton by Henry Cornish. There was also a great surge in building private houses. This was the height of the period known to historians as the 'Great Rebuilding' when many earlier houses of timber and wattle were being replaced with more substantial constructions in stone or brick where these were available. Around 1614 Alderman Thomas Brown of Woodstock used his wealth to purchase an old house and the large piece of land adjoining it, which had belonged to the Fletcher family for more than a hundred years, and built himself a new 'great house', three storeys high with a timber frame and fashionable brick infill and gabled roof. Its upper floors were reached by a wide wooden staircase of heavy construction with large wooden balls surmounting the main posts of the bannister. Other men were doing the same sort of thing in Burford, Banbury, Oxford and all the towns of Oxfordshire, where some of their houses, further altered since then, can still be found. (Part of Alderman Brown's house survives, still known as Fletcher's House, incorporated into the Oxfordshire County Museum at Woodstock.)

As part of the same process, the homes of better-off people like yeomen farmers were being enlarged and having new features incorporated such as separate kitchens (instead of the open hall), proper upper chambers reached by a staircase (instead of a mere loft with a ladder), permanent wooden panelling or 'wainscoting' and glass in the windows. All these indicated a rising standard of living for some sections of the community. One contemporary historian claimed that the period of the 'Eleven Years Tyrany' from 1629 to 1640, whatever its political implications, was one of unusual prosperity for merchants, businessmen and the larger farmers.

Towns were flourishing, but as always town life had its hazards. One of these was fire, and in spite of regulations about the use of brick for chimneys and the fashion for building in stone where it was available, there were still a large number of highly flammable timber and thatch buildings through which fire could travel rapidly in the closely packed streets of a town. Banbury suffered a particularly bad fire in March 1628, when a third of the houses in the town were destroyed in four hours. The vicar at this time was the renowned

The Falkland Arms and cottages at Great Tew. Lucius Cary, Lord
Falkland, rebuilt most of the village in the 1630s. He was later killed at the
first battle of Newbury.

puritan William Whately who saw the fire as a clear sign of God's
displeasure at the ungodly character of the town, especially the
number of malt-houses, many of which were burnt down; but in a
special sermon with the text 'Sin no more', he thanked God 'that a
part only and not the whole borough hath been consumed, and that
the greater part remaineth to succour the lesser'.

Less than twenty years later even greater damage was to be inflicted
on the town by the siege of the castle and not even that small degree of
comfort could be claimed. Disease, especially plague, was another risk
to towndwellers. In 1625 Parliament moved from London to Oxford
to escape the plague, but found Oxford little better. Many colleges had
agreements with tenants in rural parts of the county for the Fellows to
be accommodated on these farms at such times. Ordinary people who
could not afford to leave had to trust in prayers or potions, and many
died. The Revd Thomas Wyatt, Rector of Ducklington, anxiously
recorded in his journal the numbers dying of plague each week in
London, and his jottings clearly indicate the anxiety felt even in rural

areas where there was little protection against sickness. In 1639 'Many died of a new disease in Standlake', and later in the same year he reported that 'almost all the children in Ducklington and many of the married women had the measles'.

It was the numbers of inhabitants living close together and the lack of proper systems of sewerage or clean water supply that increased the dangers of living in seventeenth-century towns, but they were remarkably small by modern standards. At a time when London, by far the largest city in the country, had a population of about three hundred thousand, Oxford, including the university, had only about ten thousand. A town like Abingdon, described as 'a very populous borough and chief town of our county of Berkshire' had about 1,800 inhabitants, and Banbury with its thriving market, about 1,600. (By comparison with today this makes Oxford the size of modern Wantage, and Banbury about the same as the village of Milton-under-Wychwood.) In the seventeenth century most of England's population lived in the countryside rather than in towns.

The Oxfordshire countryside would have had a different appearance from today because most of it was made up of very large open fields and commons, three or four such areas covering a whole parish. These arable fields were divided into an apparently haphazard patchwork of interlocking furlongs served by a maze of tracks and fieldways enabling villagers to reach their scattered strips of land for cultivation. Meadows and common pasture, woodland and 'waste', which afforded rough grazing as well as fuel, made up the rest of the parish, the whole providing a much more open landscape than today. Some enclosure of parts of the open fields and commons had taken place in the interests of more profitable farming (especially sheep farming), and most parishes probably had some 'closes' near to the village, allowing individual farmers to opt out of the communal system of organizing the use of the land in the parish, but it has been estimated that only about 19 per cent of the county's land had been enclosed before 1640. Most of this was in the central vale and Chiltern areas, while in the Cotswold and redland areas in the north of the county a good deal of pasture and open field 'champion' country remained. This was rich agricultural land, its meadows beautiful in summer with a mass of wild flowers, but it was also convenient for the movement of armies and the fighting of battles and skirmishes. Troops of horse or foot-soldiers made their way across this sort of countryside unconfined by hedgerows and fenced roads, following lanes and fieldways or crossing fields and commons as it suited them, or as conditions underfoot allowed. It also favoured the kind of fighting formations used by seventeenth-century armies. In the engagement at Stow-on-the-Wold in 1643 one account describes how the parliamentary troops advanced against Rupert's forces 'marching up towards them five or six regiments together, all in a body, about eight hundred or one thousand abreast, sixe deep, we having roome enough, it being a brave champion country.' Much less convenient to ride over were the occasional rabbit warrens with carefully constructed mounds maintained by some lords. Sir William Cope of Great Milton had 80 acres of warren in 1617, from which in the previous year he had killed six hundred couples of rabbits for meat, valued at 2*s* per couple.

While there were fewer hedgerow trees there were more woods, and forests such as Wychwood covered a larger area than today. There were deer in Wychwood which the king hunted and whose skins the glovemakers of Woodstock put to good use, but timber was the most important commodity, carefully managed either as standards in great men's parks or more usually coppiced and harvested in woodland on a 7 or 10 year rotation to produce smaller dimensions.

Politically, the county was dominated by the old noble families and the gentry, who made up the establishment and served the county as MPs and Justices of the Peace. They were lords of manors and drew most of their wealth from the ownership of land. They were linked by wealth, status, class interest and often by marriage, although there was a considerable difference between those at the highest and the lowest levels of this group. Their castles and manor-houses were a feature of the countryside, symbols of their wealth and influence, and like their owners were to play a significant part in the Civil War. Beneath them in status, but not always in wealth, came rich merchants, yeomen, and professionals like lawyers and clergy. Some merchants and yeomen in particular had prospered through careful management of their resources through the years of fluctuating prices and general inflation, so that they now enjoyed considerable wealth. There was little to distinguish their possessions and lifestyle from the gentry. It was profit from wool that enabled Walter Jones to purchase the estate of the gunpowder plotter Catesby and build his beautiful house at Chastleton in the early years of the century.

Most of the rest of the population of Oxfordshire lived a long way below this level, subject to all the vagaries of life in the seventeenth-century countryside – the weather, good and bad harvests, fluctuating prices and a standard of living varying from comfortable to bare subsistence. Even craftsmen and tradesmen frequently had to combine these occupations with some small-scale farming to support themselves. They enjoyed no political power or influence beyond taking their turn as parish constable or overseer, which would involve a good deal of time attending to the needs of the poor, or simply moving them on to the next parish as quickly as possible. It might also fall to them to review the parish collection of arms rusting in the church tower, or pay expenses for the members of the local 'home guard', the trained band attending a muster. The Constable of South Newington, in his accounts for 1635, included amounts for 'the traine men at Chapel on the Hethe', 'mending the banddoles and the sords', and 'armour'. Such equipment, maintained in the parish since the days of the Armada, would suddenly become important again and would be seized by whichever side could get their hands on it first in the run up to war during the summer of 1642.

In spite of the hardships, life could still be enjoyed. There were as many as twenty-seven official holidays in the year, most of them in essence holy days reserved for religious observance, but nearly always including an element of relaxation and recreation as well. Such recreation had traditionally taken place in or around the parish church and under its auspices. The growing tide of puritan disapproval, however, had driven the traditional games and plays out of the church and into the alehouse, where they flourished. James I took a more tolerant view in his *Book of Sports* of 1618, defending traditional sports in moderation, as long as they did not actually compete with church services.

The Puritans were not alone in disapproving of alehouses. Magistrates often looked on them as a threat to the civil as well as the moral order, because they gave the lower orders of society the opportunity to meet and mingle on their own ground, to exchange ideas and express unorthodox views beyond the immediate control of the establishment. Churches were far less welcoming places to the poorer members of the community: the leaders of society sat at the front, while their servants and the poor often had to stand at the back. The alehouse was a much more congenial place. Official attempts were made to restrict their influence by forcing them to apply for a licence, those which earned a bad reputation being refused. Control was also exercised through links between magistrates and the brewers (who also were subject to the licensing system), making it difficult for unlicensed or disorderly alehouses to obtain supplies. The lower orders of society were expected to be in church on the sabbath, where they would hear improving sermons and impressive liturgy. Tippling in alehouses at the time of divine service was a constant concern of the magistrates and frequently the subject of by-laws.

Bowls, one of the most popular sports for all classes in the seventeenth century and the one most frequently mentioned by Shakespeare, was played on 'greens' in Oxford colleges, the gardens of great houses and in 'alleys' attached to alehouses. Through this last connection, as well as the practice of betting that went with it, the game acquired a disreputable image and it was one of those not approved in the *Book of Sports*. Football was also popular, but because it was often a Sunday pastime, and a very boisterous 'sport' contested between whole villages, it came in for attack by the Puritans. Charles I was apparently keen on playing football as a boy, but was advised by his father that it was too rough and unseemly for a prince. Horse-racing was more appropriate, but even here there could be violence. The annual races at Burford became famous in the seventeenth century and brought many visitors to the town, but the burial register records the death in January 1631 of Robert Tedden a stranger 'stabde with a knife by one Potley at the race', and in 1626 'William Backster gent. sometime of Norfolke and in that sheir born, and belonging to the lord Morden, was slaine at the George the next daie after the race, and was buried.'

Life for most people in seventeenth-century Oxfordshire may not have been nasty or brutish, but it was usually short. The average life expectancy at this period is said to have been about thirty-five years, a figure obviously affected by the Civil War which disrupted life for the whole population.

CHAPTER 2

WHAT THE WAR WAS ABOUT

It is not the purpose of this chapter to explore all the causes of the Civil War in depth, but merely to give a general indication of what it was that drove men to war in 1642, and to look for evidence of these issues in Oxfordshire. It is worth stating the obvious that whatever the causes, they were matters of the greatest importance to those involved at the time. While it is not too difficult to imagine going to war over the question of political authority, it is much harder for many people in Britain today to appreciate the strength of feeling that could attach to the religious issues in the seventeenth century. Which church one belongs to, (or whether one belongs to a church at all), may seem of small importance to some people today, but a glance at Northern Ireland will quickly demonstrate how much these things can still matter and how close the links between religion and politics can still be.

The political dispute was a constitutional one between the king's claim to rule by 'Divine Right', directly appointed by God and accountable only to him, and the growing demands of some of his subjects for a much greater say in the government of the country and in decision making through their representatives in Parliament. The sort of men (for in the seventeenth century it was certainly men and not women who were voicing these claims), who sought more power nationally were the gentry, prosperous yeomen and merchants whose fortunes had risen during the past two or three generations, in spite of a depression in the first decades of the seventeenth century which brought hardship to many poorer people. By using their capital to purchase land cheaply (often following the mass sale of monastic lands after the Reformation), together with careful management of resources and socially advantageous marriages, these families now found themselves wealthier perhaps than ever before. They were ambitious for a greater share in the power, status and rewards of government,

Charles I. (Gerard Honthorst, 1625)

not just at a local level where some of them already played a significant role, but on the wider national stage, either directly or at least through others whom they knew would represent their interests in the House of Commons. It has been said that the Members of the seventeenth-century Commons could have bought the Lords three times over. The supporters of such men may not have worried too much about constitutional theory, but they were concerned about the practical implications especially for trade and taxation and about their role in the local community. For many gentry and yeomen it may have been local considerations – family ties, their own position in the county community and financial interests – which influenced their choice of one side or the other when it came to war, rather than truly national issues.

Charles I's attempt to rule without Parliament from 1629 to 1640 was a threat to the influence of this class both nationally and locally. It allowed the king to impose taxes like Ship Money without their consent in Parliament, and it led to the increased use of undemocratic institutions like the Court of Star Chamber, over which local gentry had no control. Parish constables in Oxfordshire who were slow to collect their allotted share of Ship Money were summoned to London to explain themselves, not to the county Quarter Sessions.

Oxfordshire was one of the inland counties on which this tax was imposed for the first time in 1635 and there was a great reluctance to pay, partly, one suspects, because nobody likes a new tax, but also because it had not been approved by Parliament and well-known champions of opposition to the king, like John Hampden the MP for neighbouring Buckinghamshire, were active in persuading people not to pay. He and his cause were well known in Oxfordshire.

Sir George Croke of Studley Priory was one of the judges who sided with Hampden at his trial and he was strongly supported both inside and outside Parliament by William Fiennes of Broughton Castle, Lord Saye and Sele. Oxfordshire had been assessed for a total of £3,500 in 1635 (the cost of one ship of 280 tons), which was divided between all the towns and villages according to their size, but it was one of the worst counties in England for paying. Although Banbury was only ordered to find £40, (perhaps because it was still suffering from the effects of the fire in 1628), there was great difficulty in collecting it. Not for the last time, officials such as the mayor or the parish constables found themselves browbeaten by a higher authority for failing to impose on their local community a measure they did not agree with. The mayor was summoned to London and told to distrain the goods of anyone who refused to pay. In 1637 only £14 had been collected. The constables refused to collect any more, and even when some goods which had been confiscated were put on sale to raise the remainder, such was the strength of feeling and the solidarity of the local population that no one would come forward to buy it. The mayor pleaded that the citizens threatened his life when he tried to demand the tax and finally the constables were summoned to appear before the Council in London and were thrown into prison for a month. By the end of October the outstanding debt had been collected.

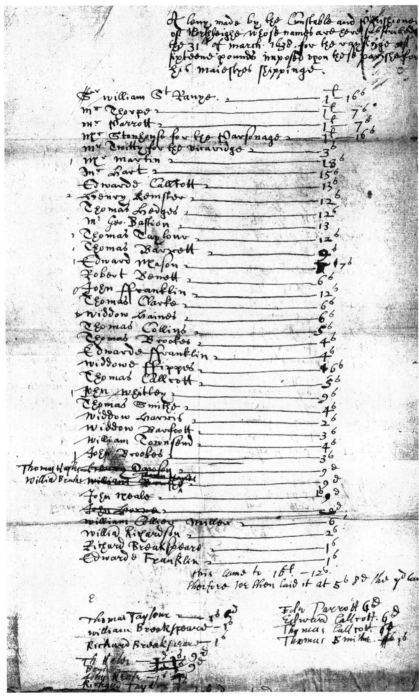

A Ship Money assessment for the parish of North Leigh, 1638. The king's
attempt to levy this tax without Parliament's consent met with strong
opposition in Oxfordshire and other counties.

Banbury was not unique, and although opposition was probably as strong there as anywhere, other towns and villages also showed great reluctance to pay. Chipping Norton was accused of being slow in meeting its assessment of £30 and it was reported that the inhabitants 'begin to disputer the extent of their liberties'. There is a clear indication here of the wider issues underlying opposition to the tax, which were soon to lead to war. The major problem for the king's government was that whatever power and authority it might claim in theory, in practice it needed the support of local officials to enforce its policies in the counties, and on the issue of Ship Money it clearly did not have this in Oxfordshire. There is a note of despair in the explanation given by the Sheriff in 1640:

> I have done my utmost to collect His Majesty's ship money, but find the county so generally adverse to pay, and all the officers so slack in execution of my warrants, that the service is very much retarded; few or none of them will pay but by distress, nor will any assist any officer therein, but threatened to sue them, and tell them a sheriff's warrant is not sufficient to bear them out; so they are thereby much disheartened. I have sent warrants according to your direction to the bailiff – for the speedy collection of the ship money – but Thomas Banister, bailiff of Dorchester Hundred, and Thomas Sterne of Thame, sent them me back again and said they would not meddle with the business. Others have proceeded to execute them but most of their distresses have been rescued from them by force, or taken out of the pound in the night; and while they are taking distress in a town the rest lock up their goods in their houses and will not sufer them to enter. Nor will any constable assist a bailiff to take a distress, but only in keeping the king's peace; nor will any man aid, or be hired to aid, in distressing; nor will any buy any distress.

It was perhaps over the religious issues that the strongest feelings were aroused. It had just about been possible up to the 1630s to contain within the Church of England a variety of quite different shades of opinion and practice which had developed since the Reformation. But the forceful policies of Archbishop Laud based on

Arminian beliefs, introduced much more radical divisions. The High Church Arminians, led by Laud and supported by Charles I, held to the doctrine of free will and salvation through repentance and the sacraments, while the rest of the church based its practice on the Calvinist belief in Predestination. The Puritans were the most fervent followers of this doctrine. Among the most significant implications of these two standpoints were their very different views about the role and status of the ministers of the church. Arminianism stressed the important role of the priest in administering the sacraments, and taught that bishops, like the king, were divinely appointed. To the Puritans, the minister's role was a more lowly one concerned with preaching and exhorting his congregation to lead Godly lives. Preaching was indeed of the utmost importance to the Puritans, and they were critical of clergy who neglected this duty, or as 'dumb curates' were too uneducated to be licensed to preach at all. Not all were dumb, however, and William Hall the curate of Bicester earned the great compliment (in Puritan terms) of being described as 'a Godly and painful preacher'. When his pluralist vicar died in 1653, Hall was allowed to succeed him with the full approval of Cromwell's commissioners. The Revd Samuel Ken, vicar of Albury and Tiddington, although a zealous Puritan, appointed curates to look after his parishes while he went off to serve as chaplain to the Earl of Essex – and to fight in his army. He was described as 'a saint in the pulpit and a devil out of it'.

While preaching also had its place in Archbishop Laud's plan for the Church, it was a restricted one. All preachers had to be licensed, which was intended to ensure not only that they had sufficient education, but also that they could be relied on not to preach unorthodox, politically dangerous interpretations of scripture. Items in the churchwardens' accounts for 1639 at Pyrton seem to hint at the efforts of Laud to bring the local churches into line and to ensure that they were fully provided with the approved books and documents:

for common prayerbookes & a booke of homilies	16*s* 4*d*
for a surplice	£2 0*s* 0*d*
for a bible	£2 14*s* 6*d*
for a booke of Articles	4*s*
for a prayer for the kinge	4*s*

The book of homilies would provide 'safe' material to be read from the pulpit in place of a sermon.

Puritan clergy like Whately of Banbury preached uncomfortable truths from within the Church, but much more radical and potentially dangerous were the unlicensed 'tub preachers', so called because they spoke to crowds assembled in the open, standing on an upturned tub or barrel – the equivalent of the modern soapbox. There were plenty of such men before 1642, but they multiplied in the Parliamentary armies once war started and were frequently the object of Cavalier mockings because of their humble origin and lack of formal education. This sarcastic comment in one of their contemporary ballads is typical:

> A multitude in every trade
> Of painful preachers you have made,
> Learned by revelation;
> Cambridge and Oxford made poor preachers,
> Each shop affordeth better teachers,–
> O blessed reformation!

Some Puritans preferred to leave England altogether. In the parish church in Chipping Norton is a memorial to the memory of William Averie, one of the bailiffs of the borough in 1634, who, following the example of the Pilgrim Fathers, emigrated to America a year later, settling at Ipswich Colony, Massachusetts Bay. Such men were driven by despair at Laud's reform of the Church in England and the desire to be part of a new community where their idea of the truth could be put into practice without fear of persecution or ridicule. Even a leading Puritan politician like Lord Saye and Sele for a time devoted his energy to founding Puritan settlements abroad rather than fighting High Churchmen at home. Together with Lord Brook he planned to emigrate, and although in the end they did not go themselves, the town of Saybrook in Connecticut was founded and named after them. They intended to allow liberty of conscience in this new 'free commonwealth', but Beesley in his *History of Banbury*, contrasts this utopian dream with the reality of Fiennes persecuting Quakers on his estate at Broughton not long afterwards, nor was the suggestion that

New England should have a hereditary aristocracy like that of the old England accepted by the settlers.

The reputation of Banbury as a hotbed of Puritanism must have owed something to the number of famous preachers operating in the area. John Dodd, originally Rector of Hanwell, became a well-known preacher at Fenny Compton and in Banbury itself where he gave weekly 'lectures' until he became Vicar of Fawsley, Northants, in 1637. By the time of the war he was an old man in his eighties, but this did not prevent Cavalier troops plundering his house. Hanwell was the family seat of the Copes, who as Puritans themselves tended to nominate leading preachers to the living, and Dodd was followed by Robert Harris, a learned divine who was consulted by Parliament on religious matters, and ended his career as Master of Trinity College, Oxford, after the war. He too was ill treated by Royalist troops quartered in his house at Hanwell before the battle of Edgehill.

The best known of all the Banbury preachers was William Whately, vicar of the parish from 1611 to 1639. He himself denied that he was an extreme Puritan, but he earned that reputation with people like the pro-Royalist antiquarian Anthony Wood for allowing typically Puritan practices such as sitting down to receive communion instead of kneeling. People used to come from as far as Oxford to hear him preach, and he dominated the Puritan scene in Banbury for many years. Wood's opinion was that 'He laid such a foundation of faction in that place that it will never be easily removed.' Sir Edward Leigh described him in more favourable terms: 'Oh with what life and zeal would he both preach and pray! and how strict and watchful was he in his whole life.' He also recalled that Whately not only urged his parishioners to give generously to the poor, but practised what he preached by regularly giving one tenth of his own income. He was clearly known throughout Oxfordshire and his death was noted by the Rector of Ducklington who wrote in his journal: 'Mr Whately an ancient famous preacher of Banbury died in May 1639.'

Abingdon's Puritan vicar was less well respected by his parishioners. Edward Roode, Vicar of St Helens was removed from his living by the Privy Council on the petition of local churchmen: 'Whereas one Mr Roode, clerk, now vicar of Abingdon, having been . . . a great disturber of the common peace . . . and publishing and delivering strange doctrines', and Puritans who tried to take down the elaborately carved screen in the church were fined 2s by the churchwardens. A few years later Henry Tesdale, the mayor, was accused of not bowing his head when the name of Jesus was mentioned in church services or kneeling to receive communion.

Such details of behaviour became the outward symbols of the fundamental differences between High Church Anglicans and Puritans. Others concerned the decoration of churches, the Puritans favouring plainness and regarding such ornaments as statues and stained-glass windows as relics of the pre-Reformation Roman Church; even carved screens and organs were condemned. They also wanted to do away with the surplice worn by priests, which regularly features in parish accounts, with an annual payment for 'washing the surplice', usually just before Christmas. Archbishop Laud's followers on the other hand, encouraged all these things as contributing to the 'beauty of holiness' which they wished to restore to church services. A particular bone of contention between the two groups concerned the position of the altar in the church. Stone altars, reminiscent of the

A communion table, Thame. It is a fine example, but was still less offensive to the Puritans than the stone altar slabs of pre-Reformation days.

Altar rails at Swalcliffe. Archbishop Laud ordered that altars should be
enclosed within rails such as these to distance them from the congregation
and to enhance the role of the priest who officiated there.

sacrifice represented by the Roman Catholic mass, should have been
removed from English churches in Elizabeth's reign and replaced by
plainer wooden communion tables. Puritans approved of this and
wished to have the table placed in the body of the church, but Laud
ordered that it should be taken back to its pre-Reformation position at
the east end, raised up on a dais and separated from the rest of the
congregation by an altar rail. Altar rails and surplices became
particular targets for Puritan zealots in the Parliamentary armies.

One of the most overt pieces of High Church symbolism in Oxford
was the new porch of the University Church of St Mary the Virgin,
erected in 1637. Its continental style, and in particular the statue of
the Virgin and Child over the door, were used as evidence of popery at
the trial of Archbishop Laud. Fear of the return of Catholicism was at
the root of much Puritan hatred of High Church practices and here
religion was inextricably linked with politics, influencing arguments
about England's foreign alliances and wars. To many Puritans, Laud
and his followers were little different from Catholics – and was not the

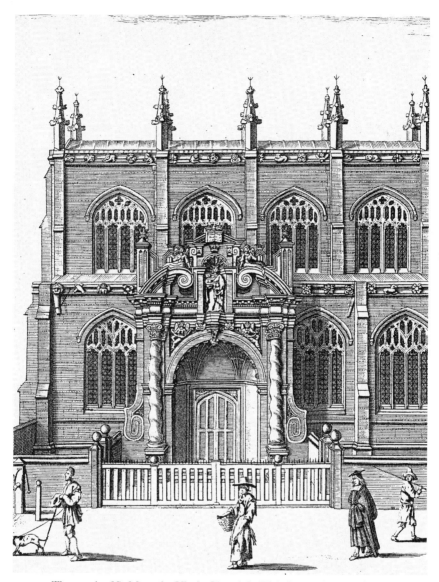

The porch of St Mary the Virgin Church in High Street, Oxford, which gave so much offence to the Puritans that Lord Saye's soldiers took pot-shots at it as they were leaving the city in 1642.

king married to a Catholic Queen who openly celebrated mass at her court?

Roman Catholics were liable to very heavy fines, but how effectively the laws were enforced depended on local sympathies. The churchwardens of Oddington made a return of recusants in their parish to the Justices at the 'twelvetide' (Epiphany) quarter sessions in 1642, and the item in their annual account: 'Spent on the ringers on gunpowder treason day . . . 1s 0d', demonstrates that 5 November was officially marked with ringing the church bells and special prayers of thanksgiving for the nation's deliverance from the Catholic plot to overthrow the government in 1605, so that it was a constant reminder to all that Catholics represented a dangerous political threat. In the main it was only wealthy Catholic families and those under their protection who could afford to continue the practice of their faith except in the utmost secrecy. Charles was suspected (not without justification) of promising to ease the restrictions on Catholics. It was partly with this in mind, as well as constitutional issues, that Parliament ordered everyone in the country over eighteen to sign a Protestation declaring that they supported 'the true Reformed Protestant Religion . . . against all Popery and Popish Innovations . . . His Majesty's Royal Person, Honour and Estate, and also the Power and Privileges of Parliaments, the lawful Rights and Liberties of the subjects'. JPs, ministers, churchwardens, constables and overseers were to make their own Protestation first – in Oxfordshire this was done at Woodstock on 14 February 1642 – and then they were to administer it to all inhabitants of their parishes over the age of eighteen. By the end of March the returns were to be sent back to the sheriff who would forward them to Westminster.

Some of the Oxfordshire returns are missing, and sadly these include both Oxford and Banbury. The separate returns for Oxford University do survive and contain a large number of names of people who claimed to be absent or too ill to be able to sign, a clear indication of the university's loyalty to the king and High Church party. The University returns also contain an amended version of the Protestation with all sorts of provisos and qualifications to the original form of words. In Henley as many as forty-five people were listed as either sick or out of town, but the parson, Robert Rainsford, expressed his confidence that they would all sign when they were able, as no one else in the parish had refused. John Phippes of Charlbury did his best to avoid committing himself to one side or the other (as many others would no doubt have preferred), the return stating that he 'simply refuseth not, but demurres upon it as pretending not to understand what is meant by the true reformed Protestant Religion'.

In Witney the excuses for not signing include 'lame', 'old and lame', 'very old and blind' and simply 'blind', but throughout the county as a whole most people appear to have signed, whether out of conviction or just for a quiet life we shall never know. In a few places the instruction that the Protestation was to be taken by everyone over eighteen was deemed to include women, but in most cases it was only thought necessary to include men.

One purpose of the Protestation was to reveal Roman Catholic recusants, and in a number of parishes there are some who openly declared themselves while in others the minister made sure that they were not overlooked even when absent: 'Mr Nappier a papist resideth at Oxford all the winter and spendeth part of the sommer at Ludwell his farme, in the parish of Wootton, neither he nor any of his servants have takn the Protestation at Wootton.'

There were a number of well-to-do Catholic families in Oxfordshire who had learned not to flaunt their Catholicism, and individuals who were able to hide it with remarkable success. The Plowdens of Shiplake Court were among these, and Thomas Plowden became a Jesuit priest, adopted a false name, and lived in the house as chaplain to his elder brother. Elizabeth Tanfield, daughter of Sir Lawrence Tanfield of Burford, married the first Viscount Falkland at the age of fifteen and soon afterwards became a Catholic, but apparently managed to keep this a secret from her husband for nineteen years! Perhaps he wondered why four of their daughters became nuns on the Continent and two sons Catholic priests (or perhaps he preferred not to know). Their eldest son, however, was Lucius Cary, the Lord Falkland who was killed at the first battle of Newbury, who sought his own religious solutions and who spoke against Laud in Parliament, although he equally opposed the abolition of bishops.

In 1641 one of the sparks which undoubtedly set light to the bonfire of religious disagreement in England was the rising of Irish Catholics

against their Protestant overlords. Many Protestants were massacred
and terrible tales of the attrocities committed were repeated in
England to fuel the prejudice and hatred against all Catholics, but
Irish ones in particular. Protestant men, women and children were
shot, stabbed and slashed to death in the bitter hatred of what today
would be called 'ethnic cleansing', and in revenge Irish Catholic
families were burned in their houses. The vivid reports of such events
inevitably created panic in England and the most damning evidence
against the king was the knowledge that he was negotiating for an
Irish army to come over to support him in England. Those Irish who
did join his armies were particularly brutally treated if captured by the
other side. It is interesting, however, to find references to poor Irish
families being given relief by churchwardens in Oxfordshire parishes
in the years before the war and even during it. In Langford what
sounds like a quite generous payment of 1s 6d was made to 'a poor
Irish woman and her children' and a smaller payment to a man in
1639, and there are payments by the churchwardens of both
Oddington and Adderbury to poor Irishmen in 1643 at the height of
the war. It is known that hundreds of Irish Protestants who had
escaped the massacre with their lives but nothing else, were shipped
over to England, and some of the later entries may refer to such
people seeking relief in parishes in Oxfordshire.

Not all the 'religious' causes were about what happened in church.
Puritanism was very much concerned with all aspects of personal and
public life, on the sabbath and during the rest of the week. At the time
of the Civil War and especially during the Commonwealth which
followed, it earned the reputation of being a doctrine of prohibition.
Puritans certainly seemed to disapprove of many of the most enjoyable
aspects of ordinary people's lives, even some that were at least in part
linked to religion, from 'church ales' to traditional ways of celebrating
Christmas. Most holidays had originally been associated with religious
festivals but the Puritans felt that secular and positively ungodly
aspects such as dancing and drinking, had come to dominate them.
Even such an apparently harmless and charming tradition as dancing
around the maypole on May Day aroused their strongest disapproval,
and the maypoles in several parts of Banbury were cut down because
of the influential Puritan element in that town, long before they were

officially banned by the Long Parliament in 1644. The argument had been going on at a national level for some time. James I had published his *Book of Sports* in 1618 officially defending traditional recreations so long as they were enjoyed with moderation and did not interfere with church services. Puritan objections on moral grounds found some support from the merchants and tradesmen who, as employers, were keen to see the number of public holidays reduced, in order to strengthen the work ethic and increase output. In Charles I's reign Sunday observance became a big issue, like so many other things symbolizing the differences between High Anglicans and Puritans. The *Book of Sports* was reissued in 1633 and was promoted by Laud, who ordered all clergy to observe it. It was so hated by Puritans that the Long Parliament ordered it to be burnt in 1643, and in the following year banned not only maypoles but all Sunday trading, sports and games, and other public holidays were eventually abolished.

Banbury was a byword for Puritan zeal throughout the country, its reputation being sufficiently widespread for satirical references to appear in plays and cartoons in London. The parish registers resound with biblical and other pious names – Ezekiel Eales, Zachery Strong, Christian Neale, Gabriell Gubbin, Hopestill Hartlett and Aholiab West (the mayor). As long ago as 1602 the famous Banbury Cross had been pulled down on the orders of the mayor, because people used to doff their caps to it and this was considered a popish superstition.

Banbury was only the most famous Puritan centre, but it is clear that several other Oxfordshire towns had strong Puritan elements. The Mayor of Oxford and the majority of the City Council, even during the war, voted to reward a public preacher 'particularly in regard to four sermons preached against swearing' – undoubtedly a brave act for a preacher in a Cavalier garrison town! It was easy to ridicule the solemn, killjoy Puritans in the seventeenth century, and their righteous message was probably never a popular one with the mass of people, rich or poor.

The Civil War was not overtly a 'class war'; aristocrats and common men fought on both sides and the issues at stake were not class ones. It was more a war between two opposing branches of the ruling classes of seventeenth-century England, a clash between the

A nineteenth-century cartoon ridiculing the strict Puritanism of Banbury. A long-faced Puritan is shown 'hanging his cat on Monday for killing a mouse on Sunday'.

absolutism of the king and the interests of those sections of society represented in Parliament. Both sides would have claimed to be the protectors of the common man in a paternalistic way, but neither had any thought of sharing power with ordinary people. Only a handful of radicals outside the mainstream of political thought held such views before 1642, but the war was to give their ideas much more publicity and support among the ordinary people who did most of the fighting, so that when the fighting was over a new element emerged in the vacuum created by the execution of the king. Even though there were men of all classes on each side, in the seventeenth century there was always a clear distinction between them, and Cavaliers in particular were disdainful of some of the Parliamentarians who had trading or similar backgrounds.

> . . . now the King and the Crown
> Are tumbling down
> And the realm doth groan with disasters;
> And the scum of the land
> Are the men to command
> And our slaves are become our masters.

There was plenty of potential for social unrest in the seventeenth century because of adverse economic circumstances, such as the steady rise in population, enclosure of land for sheep raising, fluctuating prices and general inflation, food shortages and unemployment. Those with capital to cushion them against the worst effects or even to allow them to exploit the situation survived, but others suffered real hardship. Large numbers of 'sturdy beggars' or impotent poor were a common feature of the period. Those in authority sought to deal with the symptoms of this situation by ordering harsh, even brutal, treatment of unlicensed beggars. Large numbers of landless, unemployed and dissatisfied people caused tensions in society which the war was likely to unleash. The outbursts of the Levellers and Diggers after the war were based on feeling which had been present long before it started, although they were not in themselves causes of it.

CHAPTER 3

1642: OPENING MANOEUVRES AND THE FIRST BATTLE

Oxfordshire men were to be found in prominent positions on both sides of the rapidly escalating dispute between King and Parliament. For some their strongly held religious convictions made the choice easy, but for others the decision to support one side or the other was the result of much agonizing. Undoubtedly the great majority of people, not directly involved in politics at Westminster, hoped that war could be avoided and even if it could not, that they would be able to stay out of it. By 1642 such hopes were becoming increasingly unlikely. Bulstrode Whitelock wrote in his diary that 'the times began to appear very dreadfull, and all discourses were of the threatening Civill Warre'. He also described the effect of all this on his wife who was expecting their seventh child, and 'being very neer her time of childbirth, was the more frightened att the preparations for Warre, but being of a gallant spirit and affected to the Parlement she did the better endure it'.

Whitelock himself lived at Fawley Court near Henley where he had also bought another large house, Phyllis Court. The son of a judge, he trained as a lawyer and became an MP, building up a lucrative practice through the influence of his father and his own connections. In the Commons he was clearly identified with the opposition to the king, being prominent in the prosecution of Charles's chief adviser the Earl of Strafford. In 1642 he was one of the Deputy Lieutenants for Oxfordshire and was active in the build-up to war supporting both John Hampden and Lord Saye and Sele in the early manoeuvres through which they sought to get control of the county and the city for Parliament. As a consequence his house at Fawley was ransacked by Royalist troops in the following year and he included a graphic

Bulstrode Whitelock. He was a prominent Parliamentary
lawyer and owner of Fawley Court and Phyllis Court
near Henley. (artist unknown, 1634)

description of the damage they did in his diary, which gives much
firsthand information, not just about this event, but about the politics
of the war years generally.

Bulstrode's wife clearly shared his allegiance to the Parliament
cause, but not all families were so fortunate. Sir John Cartwright of
Aynho Park also supported Parliament, but his wife remained a
Royalist. The best known example of a family with divided loyalties is
the Verney family of Claydon, just over the Buckinghamshire border.
Sir Edmund Verney, in spite of disagreeing with many of Charles's
policies, felt obliged to join the Royalist side out of a sense of loyalty

and financial indebtedness to him as king, while his son Ralph supported Parliament. The father's much-quoted words justifying his decision show clearly what mixed feelings many people had when it came to choosing sides: 'I have eaten his bread and served him near thirty years, and will not do so base a thing as to forsake him; and choose rather to lose my life (which I am sure to do) to preserve and defend these things which are against my conscience to preserve and defend.'

In the case of the Croke family at Studely Priory, Sir George Croke was an ardent Parliamentarian, having defended John Hampden at his trial for refusing to pay Ship Money, whereas his son Thomas became a Royalist with the result that the estates of a once-loyal family were for a time sequestrated by Parliament. Sir Robert Dormer, who built a new house at Rousham just before the war, had also refused to pay Ship Money, but when Pym's supporters in the Commons became more and more extreme in their opposition to the king he left them, and when war broke out he supported the Royalists. His original family seat at Ascot, Great Milton, was attacked by Hampden, while later in the war the new house at Rousham was seriously damaged by Cavalier raiders, probably because his son (another Sir Robert) inclined to Parliament.

No such doubts or divisions afflicted the Fiennes family in their ancestral home at Broughton Castle near Banbury. William Fiennes became the eighth Baron Saye and Sele in 1613, and then first Viscount in 1624. He was a convinced Puritan and opponent of both James I and Charles I in the House of Lords. Imprisoned briefly by James, he continued to object to Charles's attempts to raise money without the consent of Parliament, and became the figurehead and chief instigator of the Parliamentary opposition to the king. Broughton Castle provided a secluded meeting place for men like Pym, Hampden, Lord Brook and other leaders, but even there it was necessary to observe the greatest secrecy, the meetings taking place in the 'room that hath no ears' in a distant part of the castle where even the servants were not allowed to know the identity of the visitors. Because of his key role in coordinating the opposition to Charles in and out of Parliament, William Fiennes earned the nickname 'Old Subtlety'. The king even appointed him a Privy Councillor in 1641, attempting to win his support, an office which Fiennes accepted, but without changing his allegiance. He was one of the most influential men in Oxfordshire, his eldest son James was the county's MP while Nathaniel his second son represented Oxford city. The family had a considerable local following in the Banbury area with its strongly Puritan reputation, and after his appointment as Lord Lieutenant of Oxfordshire and Gloucestershire during the late summer of 1642 Lord Saye raised a local regiment to fight for Parliament.

At sixty when the Civil War started, he was too old to fight himself, but his sons John and Nathaniel, and his grandson Francis, did so. They too fulfilled their obligation as members of a noble family by raising troops. This meant using their influence with their tenants and other local men to persuade them to sign on, and then using their own money to meet the considerable cost of clothing and equipping them. In Lord Saye's case, if he raised a regiment of full strength, this could be as many as 1,200 men. The Troops of Cavalry raised by his sons would have consisted of about sixty horsemen with supporting saddlers and farriers. Lord Saye's regiment was uniformed in blue coats and wore the orange sash of the Parliamentary army over this. Nathaniel Fiennes was soon promoted to colonel and had a reputation as a brave officer in the early engagements.

William Lenthall, MP for the borough of Woodstock, was another who had no difficulty deciding which side he was on. Born in Henley and educated at Lord Williams's Grammar School at Thame, and at Oxford which he left without a degree, he then entered Lincoln's Inn and trained in law like many other leading men of this period. He married a daughter of John Hampden and had a successful career, apparently earning as much as £2,500 a year by the 1630s. This wealth enabled him first to purchase a house at Besselsleigh near Abingdon in 1630 and then, in 1634, Burford Priory and the lordship of Burford, for which he paid £7,000. He became MP for Woodstock before the end of James I's reign, was a keen defender of the rights of Parliament and was elected Speaker of the House of Commons at the beginning of the Long Parliament in 1640, a post which eventually made him one of the most important men in the country, as the official voice of Parliament. He is best remembered for his famous response as Speaker, to Charles' unconstitutional invasion of the

William Fiennes, Lord Saye and Sele. Known as 'Old
Subtlety', he played a leading part in the opposition to
Charles I both nationally and locally.

House when he tried to arrest the five members who led the
opposition to his policies. When the king demanded to know where
they were, he replied that he had 'neither eyes to see nor tongue to
speak in this place but as the House is pleased to direct me, whose
servant I am here'.

Lenthall had purchased Burford from Lucius Cary, Viscount
Falkland, who had inherited considerable debts from his father so
that he was forced to sell half of the family's Oxfordshire estates.
The half he kept was the manor of Great Tew, renowned in the
seventeenth century as it is in the twentieth, for its peacefulness and
picturesque appearance, which Falkland did much to enhance. He
started the process of buying back the freeholds and may have

rebuilt most of the houses in the village using the local ironstone with thatch on the roofs and details like the drip-moulds and stone mullions, some of which are still such a feature of the village today, in spite of later restoration. To his Jacobean manor-house with its walled gardens, he attracted many of the leading men of the day: Edward Hyde, later Earl of Clarendon, loyal minister to Charles II and author of the first full account of the Civil War, Ben Jonson the playwright, Edmund Waller the poet, Sir Kenelm Digby the philosopher, scientist and courtier, and John Selden, an outstanding scholar and writer on legal history as well as being MP for Oxford University. Perhaps at no time before the present has the tiny village of Great Tew been so well known as in the decade before the outbreak of the Civil War, when it was a centre of peaceful discourse and enlightenment. While just a few miles away at Broughton political leaders met in deadly secret to plot their opposition to the king's ministers, others were gathering at Tew to escape from the heat of politics into a rural retreat where music, art and literature were more likely to be the subjects for discussion.

Lucius Cary himself was one of those who had often found himself arguing against the king. He had denounced Ship Money as unconstitutional and had been against some of Archbishop Laud's High Church innovations, but when the Parliamentary opposition began to propose more extreme measures like the abolition of bishops, he felt that they were going too fast and too far for him, and so ended up as a prominent Royalist when it came to war. In January 1642 Charles appointed him Secretary of State, and in that position he tried hard to avert war by seeking some kind of religious compromise, but it was too late.

Anthony Wood, at ten years old, was too young to take part in the war in 1642, but he seems to have taken a great interest in it and it is to him that we owe much of our knowledge of events and conditions in Oxford. In 1674 he published his *History and Antiquities of the University of Oxford* which included an account of the war years in Oxford seen very much from the point of view of a Royalist member of the university. Even allowing for his bias and the fact that it was written some time after the events it describes, it is an invaluable record. Because of the disruption and danger in Oxford his parents

Lucius Cary, Lord Falkland.

sent him to Thame, where he lodged with the vicar and studied as a pupil at Lord Williams's Grammar School and nonetheless managed to witness some of the action.

The war did not only affect the prominent figures in the county who had a part in national politics. Much more ordinary folk also held strong views, and even those who kept their views to themselves or had no views at all, were caught up in the escalating tensions and the inevitable move to open warfare. Wyatt noted that the Puritans were 'grown very odious and are now called of all Round heades'. Men who over the past few years had gone off once or twice to attend a muster of the local Trained Bands, perhaps laughed and jeered at by their wives or others in the parish who resented the cost to the community, suddenly found that control of these same Trained Bands – the only trained soldiers in England apart from some who had seen service in foreign wars – was a matter of the greatest importance and the cause of the first blows being struck between the rival parties rapidly forming in every county. In March 1642 Parliament issued its Militia Ordinance, putting the Trained Bands under the control of Lord Lieutenants. In Oxfordshire it then proceeded to appoint Lord Saye as Lord Lieutenant in place of the Earl of Berkshire, and he began raising troops for Parliament. Months later, on 16 August, the two sides clashed at Watlington when the earl as the King's Commissioner for Array tried to summon all loyal subjects in Oxfordshire to answer the king's call to arms. He was prevented by a body of men under John Hampden accompanied by Bulstrode Whitelock, his coach was smashed and he was unceremoniously sent off to London as a prisoner.

There had already been a much bigger confrontation in the north of the county between Lord Brook and the Earl of Northampton. Brook, as their appointed Lord Lieutenant for Warwickshire, had orders from Parliament to strengthen the defences of Warwick by taking six cannons there from Banbury Castle. When he set out with the guns, guarded by about a hundred men and a cheering crowd of gentlemen and others from the town, he was unexpectedly stopped by a much larger force headed by the Earl of Northampton, who was intent on seizing them for the king. Lord Brook was saved by the amount of support for Parliament in the Banbury area. Hundreds of men turned out from all the neighbouring villages, hastily armed with staves, billhooks or whatever weapons they could grab, and rushed to swell the ranks of his tiny force. 'The country came in very thick . . . women also came to his company bringing in Beere and Victuall in aboundance and six or seven cartloads of harrowes to welcome their horses.' Northampton seems to have been taken aback by this sudden assembly, and both commanders were obviously reluctant to cause the first bloodshed. Instead their men glared at each other and shouted threats while the leaders parleyed and finally came up with an amazing 'gentleman's agreement' which allowed Brook to go back to Banbury with the guns but to promise that he would give three days'

Lord Williams's Grammar School, Thame, was attended by some of the
leading figures of the day including John Hampden and the antiquarian
Anthony Wood.

notice before trying to move them out again. The Earl of
Northampton for his part agreed to warn Lord Brook with the same
three days' notice before he attempted to attack him in Banbury. It
was the last time that differences were settled by discussion rather than
by fighting, and indeed it was already too late for such an attempt to
succeed for long. Lord Brook having gone back to London,
Northampton's men spent the next week frightening the people of
Banbury with talk of massive reinforcements coming to attack them,
while at the same time luring away their supporters who had come
from the surrounding area by making them think their own homes,
wives and families were in danger. Nothing demonstrates more clearly
the inexperience of those involved at this early stage of the war than
their behaviour in this episode.

People poured out of Banbury in panic, unsure where to run for
safety and the Royalists crept in under cover of darkness. The
following morning they summoned John Fiennes and his garrison in
the castle to hand over the six cannon or they would set fire to the

town. For the inexperienced and frightened garrison and their young leader this threat was enough. The guns were apparently surrendered without a struggle and carried off in triumph to the Earl of Northampton's seat at Compton Wynyates.

News of these events spread quickly throughout the county bringing excitement to some and consternation to others, while everyone attempted to make whatever preparations they thought might serve in this unprecedented situation. In Oxford the deputy vice-chancellor took very positive action by forming a university regiment made up of 'privileged men' (the tradesmen and employees serving the university who had a special status within the city) and a number of the scholars who enthusiastically joined in the muster held at 'the schools'. Anthony Wood's descriptions of these early parades are reminiscent of the Home Guard at the outset of the Second World War. There were no uniforms and a shortage of equipment led to sets of armour being shared, and antiquated weapons such as bows and arrows being resurrected. 'Mr Wood's father had then armour or furniture for one man, viz. a helmet, back and breastpiece, a pyke and a musquet, and other appurtenances: and the eldest of his menservants . . . did appear in those armes when the scholars and privileged men trained, and when he could not train, as being taken up with business, the next servant did traine.'

These raw but enthusiastic recruits paraded for training every few days during August, marching through the streets to the New Parks to be put through their drill which on 20 August consisted of being 'divided into foure squadrons, whereof two of them were musketers, the third was a squadron of pikes, the 4th of hallberdes; and after they had beyn reasonably instructed in the wordes of commaund and in their postures, they were put into battell arraye, and skirmished together in a very decent manner'. When they came back into the town they were marched from the North Gate, along Cornmarket Street to Carfax and down the High Street 'so both towne and country might take notice thereof' before being dismissed. There was a sense of bravado about all this and the whole atmosphere was far removed from the realities of war. The training on one day was cut short because the weather was 'something unseasonable and wet' and 30 August was 'all daye wett, and nothinge done'. On one occasion the parades were watched by two of the King's Commissioners who had not been captured at Watlington, Lords Wilmot (of Adderbury) and Lovelace, but they were apparently so nervous about being kidnapped by Parliament supporters that they watched discreetly from a window.

King Charles formally raised his royal standard at Nottingham on the 22nd at a rather inauspicious ceremony when it was blown down by the strong wind. Failing to gather enough support there he headed north to York, but being assured of the loyalty of Oxford University and also aware of the strong Puritan element in the area, he sent a detachment of troops under Sir John Byron to secure the city. These men had a rough time around Brackley where they were attacked and harassed by the locals with their pitchforks and billhooks so seriously that a number of men and horses were killed. Byron was carrying with him his commission from the king addressed to the City and University of Oxford, a large sum of money and some personal belongings. For greater safety he decided to send these on separately in the care of a servant who he hoped would be able to pass unnoticed through the lanes and byways, thus making his way to Oxford. The unfortunate man managed to lose his way, however, and hiding Byron's parcel in a field of oats near the present Pimlico Farm between Croughton and Fringford, wandered into Croughton where he was immediately spotted as a suspicious stranger and forced to reveal all. He and the treasure were gleefully seized and carried off to Banbury Castle by some Parliament soldiers. Byron's frustration and embarrassment can be sensed in an angry letter he wrote to 'Master Clarke at Croughton' in which he huffed and puffed and threatened retribution on Mr Clarke's estates if the goods were not returned.

The scholars in the university regiment were no doubt enjoying their novel experience which included doing all-night guard duty at the entrances to the city. The unexpected arrival at midnight on 28 August of Byron's tired troops, having made their way from the troubles at Brackley, caused considerable alarm, both to them and to the inhabitants. The university feared they might be Parliamentarians while the City Council, whose participation in the mustering of soldiers for the king had been very half-hearted, were equally afraid of a strong Royalist presence. Indeed, so great was their fear that a number of prominent Parliament sympathizers made a hasty escape to Abingdon. Among them was Alderman John Nixon, perhaps the best known of the anti-Royalist members of the Council. His flight was noticed with disapproval by some who stayed at their posts, and three weeks later his colleagues declined to elect him mayor in spite of the backing of Lord Saye and Sele.

Byron stayed in Oxford for ten days during which his men assisted with the defensive works being undertaken by the university in order to preserve the city for the king. That the townspeople were not so keen on this objective was obvious when their own Trained Band militiamen confronted soldiers who were about to break down the bridge on the causeway to Botley and prevented them replacing it with a drawbridge.

It was soon the turn of the university to be afraid of reprisals, as news came that a large Parliamentary force was approaching from Aylesbury. Suddenly the Deputy Vice-Chancellor was anxious for Byron to leave, and went himself to plead with Lord Saye that they had now laid down their arms and sent the troops away. He got short shrift, however, being taken as a delinquent and sent to London to answer to Parliament. Meanwhile Byron left Oxford and headed north but was warned that John Fiennes' troop of horsemen was lying in wait for him at Chipping Norton. He hired a local man in Woodstock to show him a back way by which he could avoid Fiennes, but whether he did or not, the Woodstock man was apparently caught by Fiennes near Enstone and 'well whipped naked for his paines'.

The Parliament forces from Aylesbury reached Oxford on 12 September, presented their commission to the mayor in the name of Parliament and were admitted. Only in the early stages of the war would such formalities have been observed. Lord Saye himself made a formal entry in his coach with an escort of soldiers at five o'clock that afternoon. He immediately gave orders that the ditches and other defences constructed by the scholars should be filled in (and no doubt required the stones taken up to the roof of Magdalen Tower for dropping on the heads of advancing Parliamentarians to be carried down again). That night 'somewhat late' he went to New College and The Queen's with a guard of soldiers with flaming torches to search for weapons and silver plate which he suspected had been hidden away. Dr Fell, Dean of Christ Church, was caught trying to send a trunk of goods out of the college by a back way, and sure enough quantities of the college's silver were discovered secreted behind some panelling and more in the cellar. The soldiers were everywhere in the next few days, searching college buildings and private houses and seizing arms and money. One of the fellows of Oriel was foolish enough to say that he would rather lend the king £1,000 than lend 1*d* to Parliament, and was promptly thrown into prison and two brothers were angrily punished for crying 'a poxe on all Roundheads', one of them being taken to Woodstock and 'whipped through the regiment'. Lord Saye satisfied his Puritan zeal by organizing a bonfire in the street and publicly burning a selection of 'Popish books and pictures' which had been seized from churches and houses in the area.

There was much confusing coming and going of troops during the rest of September. By the end of the month there were as many as three thousand in the city and it was no doubt beginning to feel much less enjoyable for the townspeople who had to accommodate them and put up with their rough behaviour which was not always in keeping with the traditional image of a Puritan. After a bout of drinking and taunting each other, two rival regiments got into a serious fight up and down High Street and Carfax, a number being injured by having thumbs and fingers cut off. Lord Saye himself had trouble with them when they demanded pay that was overdue and became mutinous. Officers, soldiers and civilians were beginning to experience some of the problems which would become everyday occurrences over the next four years.

On the 23rd the first skirmish had been fought between soldiers from the two main armies at Powick Bridge near Worcester and the real war was moving closer to Oxfordshire. Men, and women, who only weeks ago had excitedly flocked to support Lord Brook at Banbury and to shout abuse at his opponents, or who had laughed at the clumsy manoeuvres of the scholars training to be soldiers in Oxford, were suddenly realizing that the comic aspect of the situation was fast disappearing, and they were about to be caught up in something much less pleasant.

At this point Lord Saye made what has sometimes seemed a surprising and short-sighted decision to leave Oxford unguarded. He summoned all the heads of colleges and lectured them about their behaviour in the past and ordered them not to give further assistance to the Royalists. He even returned most of the confiscated plate in return for an assurance that it would not be used in support of the king. He then marched all his troops out of the city leaving it to its own devices. Knowing how important Oxford and its wealth was to be to Charles throughout the rest of the war, people have often wondered why Lord Saye left it without a garrison. Bulstrode Whitelock was with him and, with others, urged him to hold on to it. It was likely that Whitelock himself would have become governor of Oxford, and his own opinion was that Lord Saye abandoned it because he did not like this idea. More plausible is the strategic argument that he could not afford to leave a large part of his forces tied down in Oxford when they would be more use strengthening the Parliamentary army commanded by the Earl of Essex in preparation for the major battle that all could see was about to be fought somewhere in the Midlands.

Both main armies were gathering supplies and reinforcements from all parts of the country ready for this encounter. On 15 October Wyatt saw the Mayor of Worcester and an alderman with a load of plate and silver pass through Ducklington on the way to London via Abingdon in order to swell the coffers of Parliament, and on the same day he noted three or four hundred soldiers and eight loaded wagons going through in the other direction. A week later '3 hundred and more of foote soldiers came through Ducklington and lodged at Witney. They came from Portsmouth etc.'

The Battle of Edgehill was fought on Sunday 23 October 1642. It took most of the day to get the armies formed up in their fighting positions, the Royalist infantry being some miles away when the site for the battle was chosen by the king. The story of the battle has been told elsewhere many times. Its best known feature is Prince Rupert's ill-disciplined but fearsomely effective headlong cavalry charge which swept all before it, but was unable to stop itself so that his cavalry was removed from the battle for most of the rest of the day while they hallooed and hunted after the fleeing Roundheads, cutting them down with their swords with no more mercy than they showed to fox or deer, and then merrily plundering the Parliamentary baggage wagons and chasing off the terrified women camp followers. This left one wing of

The view from Edgehill, scene of the first major battle of
the Civil War in October 1642.

the king's army unprotected and the Parliamentary forces were able to
redress the balance here, but inexperience and weariness meant that
by the end of the day neither side could claim victory. As darkness fell
on that cold October day, both armies drew back in sheer exhaustion,
but their commanders would not let them leave the field and appear
to admit defeat, nor dare they move forward to rescue the dying or
remove the bodies of those already dead. Each having withdrawn a
little way, they stood to their stations all night, suddenly shivering with
cold after the heat of battle, hungry and exhausted, listening to the
shouts and moans of the wounded in the darkness in front of them,
and realizing, perhaps for the first time, what war was really like. As
dawn broke on a hard frost both armies faced each other again but
the only movement either made was the king sending forward a party
to recover some guns. Later on in the day the Earl of Essex withdrew
his troops rather than renew the fight. Fifteen hundred men died.

The suffering of the non-combatants was also great. Armies did not
suddenly appear on the scene, fight a battle and go away again. For
days before and after Edgehill the thousands of soldiers involved in the
two armies were moving about the area, foraging for food, drink,
lodging, fodder for horses, wagons to carry their goods and anything

else they wanted. Many hundreds of wounded and badly maimed soldiers were left behind in Kineton and other villages to be cared for by the local people if they would, or to fend for themselves if they could. Clarendon says that wounded Royalists unfortunate enough to be stranded in the strongly Puritan locality were clubbed to death by villagers. There was also considerable loss of livestock and damage to fields from the battle itself and the movement of troops. Oxfordshire was fortunate that it was spared from the immediate effects of a battle on this scale, as nothing like it was fought in the county.

News of the battle travelled fast, but tended to be incomplete and sometimes innaccurate. Inhabitants of Warwickshire villages as much as 20 miles away heard the noise while they were at church on the Sunday and went to see the sight and find out what had happened. Some of them were caught up in the fighting and badly wounded as a result. The beacon on the Avon Dassett hills was lit by Parliamentarians after the battle, so that its light could be seen as far away as Ivinghoe in Buckinghamshire and the message passed to London claiming a victory. There was still some uncertainty nearer to the scene, however, and messengers were dispatched to London to find out the official verdict because there were so many rumours. They were informed that Parliament had had a great deliverance and a little victory. Wyatt heard that the king had won a victory near Edgecote and that ten thousand had been killed. Anthony Wood's account mentions two or three great fights having taken place on 22, 23 and 24 October.

Rejecting the advice of Rupert and some others that he should immediately speed towards London and press home any advantage the battle had given him, Charles instead decided to take Banbury Castle, which had been his intention before the battle. It apparently offered little resistance to the greatly superior forces now brought against it and was occupied on the 27th. There was some surprise and even a suggestion of treachery among the garrison to account for the ready surrender of such an important and strong castle, but the troops handed over not only the castle but its store of arms, ammunition, clothing and other equipment, all of which was a great bonus to an army which had just used up or lost much of its own supplies in a major battle. Broughton Castle had also surrendered to the king, which must have been a matter for much celebration among the enemies of the Fiennes family. Both the long-suffering town of Banbury and the castle at Broughton are said to have been plundered by Prince Rupert's men, but there is disagreement as to whether this was with the king's approval or not. The young Sir William Compton was made governor of the Banbury garrison and held it until the last year of the war.

The king now moved to his palace at Woodstock and then on 29 October made a triumphant entry into Oxford, the army marching with all their colours and those captured from the enemy at Edgehill. He was enthusiastically welcomed by the university at Christ Church and one imagines less warmly by the mayor and Council, although they did make him a traditional gift of money at Penniless Bench. The army was found quarters in and around Oxford and Rupert established a base for his cavalry, said by Wood to number four thousand, at Abingdon where the bells were rung as a sign of loyalty both on the 29th and again two days later when the prince himself arrived. It seems that the town's churches were used as quarters for some of the troopers and the churchwardens had to make payments for cleansing them on several occasions, once trying to get rid of the smell by purchasing incense.

At this date Oxford was only looked on as a temporary staging post on the way to London which was the main objective, and within a few days Charles set off again through Abingdon towards Reading, which was taken on 3 November. Just over a week later the defending Parliamentarians were easily driven out of Brentford and the population was severely pillaged by Rupert, so badly that a little later when friendly troops returned it was reported that the innkeepers were begging bread from the soldiers. The king's advance was finally stopped at Turnham Green where the London Trained Bands under Skippon blocked their way. By the end of November the king and his army were back in Oxford.

Having failed in his immediate plan to take London and end the war at a stroke, it now became necessary to secure his base at Oxford not only by constructing physical defences around that city, but by establishing garrisons in all the main towns and manor houses around it. The obvious danger was on the eastern side where a counter-attack by the Earl of Essex was expected sooner or later. Reading had just been occupied and was held by a garrison, and another was put into Wallingford. This town was held for the king throughout the entire war with unfailing loyalty and great vigour by Thomas Blagge, a Suffolk gentleman who raised a regiment for the king and was appointed colonel. He greatly strengthened the defences of the medieval castle and built a drawbridge across the Thames so that the town became an impregnable fortress and a base for raids on the surrounding countryside. The other Thames crossing was defended by Abingdon under the governorship of Lord Wilmot. Henley, in spite of its connection with both Speaker Lenthall and Bulstrode Whitelock, was taken over by Royalist troops, but not fortified. Two well-remembered events took place here in November one of which was the capture of a Roundhead spy who was ordered by Rupert to be hanged. The sentence was carried out using an elm tree which for ever after was known as Rupert's Elm, (and apparently lived for well over 300 years). A little before this, when Rupert's forces first entered the town, a detachment under Sir John Byron occupied Bulstrode Whitelock's house at Fawley Court. His youngest children, the oldest of whom was only six and the youngest a baby of a few months, were being cared for by one of Whitelock's tenants who tried to pass them off as the children of his servant. Byron saw through this attempt, but treated the children gently and left them in peace. His troops, however, behaved very differently towards Whitelock's property at Fawley Court where a great deal of damage was done to the house, his books and papers and to his park. Such was the fate of prominent men's houses on both sides when their homes fell into the hands of the enemy.

As the winter deepened the fighting did not stop. Wilmot led an expedition out of Oxford at the beginning of December ranging as far south as Marlborough which was seen by the king as a threat to Oxford's supplies both of corn and cloth from that area, both vital to the army. Roundhead troops from Northamptonshire made a bid to recapture Banbury Castle just before Christmas when they heard that its governor had gone out of the town towards Oxford. The castle's walls and gate proved too strong even when guns were fired at them from close range, and when Prince Rupert came from Oxford on 23 December with a relieving force the Roundheads withdrew.

Troops were still being sent in and out of Oxford throughout the Christmas period, but no doubt the townspeople did their best to celebrate the festival in the increasingly overcrowded conditions of their city. There were royal celebrations in Christ Church, and on 27 December both the king and Rupert played real tennis in Oxford's new court. Their game was interrupted on the 28th by the arrival of a trumpeter sent as a messenger from the Parliament in London to seek a safe conduct for their representatives who wished to come to Oxford to discuss peace. Charles received the trumpeter in the tennis court and agreed to the talks.

CHAPTER 4

OXFORD: THE DIVIDED CITY

The year 1642 saw many comings and goings in Oxford, with attempts to secure the city for both sides. In the autumn the king arrived to stay, and Oxford's status and place in history as the Royalist capital was assured. Although an important town because of its university, it was by no means as large and commercially successful as other alternative capitals such as York or Bristol. Oxford did have several attributes, however, that made it an obvious choice. First, its location, in the heart of England, enabled the king to threaten communications between London and the Parliamentary garrisons. The ring of outer defences guarded communications with the north at Banbury, while Donnington Castle guarded the southern routes. Oxford was only 50 miles from London, which Charles had by no means despaired of retaking, using Oxford as a base. Second, Oxford could provide accommodation. The university and college buildings offered Charles lodgings for himself, his family and the court in suitably grand surroundings. To an extent, Oxford was used to visitors, with the townspeople running lodging houses and providing services for the university such as laundry and supplies of food. Finally, there was Oxford's wealth. The colleges had substantial quantities of gold and silver plate and the city's tradespeople included many very wealthy men and women – among them Thomas Dennis, Humphrey Whistler and Martin Wright. The king desperately needed money to finance his armies. The setting up of the mint and collection of gold and silver to provide for the new coins was one of Charles' first actions.

Oxford fulfilled a vital role in providing a settled, secure base from which to command operations, and this was recognized by the enemy. In 1646, when the taking of Oxford by Parliament became of paramount importance, the Parliamentary commander Fairfax wrote to Parliament 'that the reducing of this city of Oxford [is] to be of great Concernment to the Whole Kingdom and of great use to the Peace thereof, it being the Mother Seat to hold up the spirit of the Enemy.'

Preparations for war had begun in Oxford as early as spring 1642 but with the king arriving for good these reached a new intensity. The Royal Mint was established in New Inn Hall Street under the control of Thomas Bushell, who had been Master of the Shrewsbury Mint. The king established his court at Christ Church, and Queen Henrietta Maria, who arrived in July 1643, set up hers in neighbouring Merton College. A gunpowder magazine was set up in New College and the artillery itself was parked in Magdalen Grove. Anthony Wood was at school in New College at the time. The arrival of the gunpowder, placed in the cloister and tower, meant that the school removed to the choristers' chamber at the east end of the common hall. The change does not seem to have been for the better, Wood recalled: 'It was a dark nasty room and very unfit for such a purpose which made the scholars often complaine, but in vain.' The school's tower was requisitioned as an armoury from December 1642, with local gunsmiths and metalworkers being employed to repair arms and other military equipment. The following month metalworking shops in Oxford were taken over. Everyone was expected to play a part in providing for the defence of the city and the king. Contributions ranged from muskets, pikes, armour and tools to almost any metal object that could conceivably be melted down in a process that was the reverse of swords into ploughshares. In March 1643 Sir Samuel Luke, Essex's spymaster-general, received reports that one Anthony Carter, a brasier 'by vertue of a warrant to him granted by his majesty went through the towne yesterday to every howse and tooke up all the pots panns kettles and skellets they could find to make Ordinance withal'. A foundry was set up in Christ Church and another in Frewin Hall. The college walls reverberated with the unusual sounds of metal being beaten and forged. Oxford's mills were used to grind gunpowder while uniforms for the soldiers were made in the Astronomy and Music Schools.

The Royalist Ordnance papers contain receipts dating from the spring of 1643 which illustrate all this activity, as all manner of military supplies were handed in to the Ordnance Comissioners. Local people arrived almost daily with contributions. On 12 March 1643, a typical day, muskets were received from, among others, Nicholas Jinks Cooke of All Saints, Christopher Towlerbery, chandler of All Saints, Umpton Crooke Esq. of All Saints, John Walker, glover of St Peter in the Bailey, Joseph Godwyn, bookseller of St Mary Magdalen, (there is a note to say that his musket had been left him by a soldier), and Mathew Lelloe, innkeeper of St Peter in the Bailey. Thomas Williams, an innkeeper from St Michael provided a musket rest, bandoliers and a pike.

The manufacture of gunpowder was of crucial importance as many of the country's existing stocks lay in Parliamentary hands. Its manufacture had been controlled before the war using patents and monopolies. William Baber, originally from Bristol, appears to have taken charge of production in Oxford. There are receipts for varying quantities of powder, measured in weight or simply barrels, being handed over by him, presumably as fast as he could manufacture it in the city mills.

As well as the stores, the city defences had to be strengthened against attack. At this stage Oxford's medieval walls were still in existence, with entry to the centre via the four gates: north, south, east and west. Security at these entry points was tightened throughout the Royalist occupation. Some of the citizens complained about these restrictions and their detrimental effect on trade. On 26 August 1643 Sir Arthur Aston, then Oxford's military governor, gave instructions to the City Council that they were 'To have four knoweing townsmen, one at each gate, to signifie to the watch that they know this townesman or that countrie man'. There were houses lying outside the walls in the suburbs, whose occupants perhaps ranked as some of the unluckiest in Oxford. Not only did they lie outside the protection of the medieval walls, but St Clements and Wolvercote were outside even the new line of defence works. On several occasions when the Parliamentary forces came too close for comfort, the Royalists flooded pasture near the Cherwell and the Thames, and in 1644 burnt suburban settlements rather than see them commandeered as shelter for the enemy. As early as March 1643 orders were given to cut down trees and pull up hedges so that the Parliamentary soldiers might be better seen and fired upon from the city walls. The medieval walls were repaired and strengthened, having not been needed defensively for generations. New defensive bulwarks and ditches were constructed under the supervision of the Dutch engineer Bernard de Gomme. A drawbridge was set up at Magdalen Bridge. Anthony Wood recalled visiting Magdalen Bridge to see the works on 22 November 1642: 'in the afternoone I went to see the foundation laienge of the new timberworke gate uppon Magdalen's bridge, and the newe earthen wall raised from the saide bridge to the corner of the phisicke garden, to laye the peices of ordinance there, to secure the entrance uppon the bridge'. The workforce for the digging and building was supplied by both the university 'Privileged Men' and scholars, as well as the townspeople and their families. The shire also provided a proportionate share. On 5 December 1642 Anthony Wood commented, somewhat acidly, that at the university end of the works 'there were a great many (the Colledges sending forth workemen allso); and at the town worke [north of St Giles' church] there were but twelve persons only then at worke'. There should have been sixty-two. In fact there probably were only a dozen; the Oxford City Archives still has 'A note of all such that came with shovles, spades, mattocks to do service for his Majesty in and about the fortifications and bullworks of this Cittie the 2nd December 1642.' There are only fourteen names on the list! The reluctance of the townspeople to take part in the labour on the defences, a reluctance that probably stemmed from the fact that the work was unpaid and working in this way meant losing a day's labour elsewhere rather than political motives, was to cause a certain amount of royal displeasure and was just one of the points of friction between the city and its military governors.

The preparations seem to have impressed the enemy. Edward Sherwin reported to Luke on 6 March 1643 'that they are very strongly fortified and that there are 6 peeces of ordinance lye all abrest at the entrance into the citty, and that by relation there was about 3000 of the king's forces in and about the towne'. On 8 March Robert Cox told him 'that Magdalin Bridge at the entrance into Oxford is drawne upp that soe there is only passage for footemen but none for horse. And that there is a greate gate made upon Wheatley Bridge and none hardly suffered to passe without a tickett from Sir Jacob Ashley [then governor].' However, the defences do seem to have been patchy in their strength. Reports of work needing to be done on them continue throughout the occupation, which suggests they may have remained incomplete, or have needed frequent repairs. Reports of Oxford's strength fluctuate, a lot depending on the numbers of the king's forces stationed there at the time. These were part of his field army and not just a garrison for the city. Military engagements elsewhere caused many comings and goings. There were times when Oxford was left to defend itself against possible attack, its only protection being the City Regiment, recruited from townspeople and scholars and hastily trained.

Clarendon wrote in his *History of the Great Rebellion*, that Oxford was the only city in England 'that he [Charles I] could say was entirely at his devotion'. If this was so the king's situation was unhappy indeed, for even here there were those who viewed his arrival with mixed feelings. The university was basically sympathetic (though not necessarily over eager to back up this sympathy in more tangible forms). The City Council, who tended to disagree with the university on principle were less wholehearted. The City Council and university had already known centuries of competition for supremacy within the city boundaries and their rivalry was increased by the circumstances of the war. The university support for the king ensured that its star was in the ascendant, which can only have irritated the City Councillors. Throughout the occupation and indeed in the aftermath of the Civil War both sides continued to occupy themselves with disputes over their respective rights and privileges.

The City Council at this time consisted of the mayor, aldermen and others elected from the Common Council to form an inner council known as The Thirteen. The Common Council was made up of men elected from the city's freemen, who were the only people allowed to trade within the city boundaries. The Council basically represented tradespeople, merchants and craftsmen, a class that broadly speaking, tended to sympathize with the Parliamentary views on Parliamentary rights, religion and government. Whatever the feelings of those in Oxford when the king arrived, thirteen members of the Council had already left. They included Alderman John Nixon, who was certainly

Councell of warrs att Oxford 19th of Aprill 1644.

His Maty

Present

Lord Treasuror.   Duke of Richmond
Marquesse of Hertford   Lord Greate Chamblain
Lord Chamberlayne   Earle of Bristoll
Lord Dunsmore   Lord Savill
Mr Secretary Nicolas   Mr of the Rolles.

Sr Edward Nicholas

Consideracon being then taken of compleating & giving
all fitt encouragemt to the Citty Regimt. It was
thereupon ordered by his Maty by the advice of his
Councell of warre, that the said Regimt should bee
compleated to the number of 800 men in sixe
Companyes, being about 137 in a Company, of which
not above 120 to bee obliged to appeare to doe duty
every night, soe as they bee not under that number.

That duty shall bee done but by One Company in a
night, soe oure man will watch but one night in sixe.

That the freemen, & auncient Inhabitants of this Citty
shall bee of the Citty Regimt and of noe other, to which
purpose the Governor to have notice given him hereof.

It was farther ordered that all such freemen of this
Towne or other auncient Inhabitants, or their servts
who shall refuse to pay their Assessmts towards the
chargee of this Regimt (they being indifferently layed)
or shall refuse to list themselves and to doe
duty in this Regimt shall bee looked upon as persons
that thereby give just cause to the suspecion of their
Loyalty and affeccon to his Maties service, and if they
shall not speedily comply, soe that his Maty may bee
confident

Minutes of the king's council of war held in Oxford, April 1644. The
council issued instructions to the city about the raising of a City Regiment
consisting of 800 men in six companies 'being about 137 in a company, of
which not above 120 to bee obliged to appeare to doe duty every night, soe
as they bee not under that number'.

St Martins

1 willm ...
2 willm ...
3 William Hall 1 pike
4 ...
5 ...
6 ...
7 James Dalby
8 ...
9 Edw. ...
10 Jo. Cobb
11 Richard ...
12 ...
13 ... Bullock ...
14 Jo. ...
15 Robte Langley a pike
16 Richard Well
17 Robte ...
18 ...
19 ...
20 Jo: Dabs
21 ...
22 Richard ...
23 ...
24 Richard Ireland
    Edward ... pike a musket
25 Martin ...
26 ... Bradford
27 James ... a pike
28 ... a musket
29 ... White a pike
    ... Bradford pike
    ... drummer

Workmen of
Captayne Bowmans

James Rose
John Cooley
Francis Powell
Henr White
Thomas Browne
John Cobb
Edward Badger
Robert ...
Edward Hart
Thomas Simpson
John ...
Wm Harrison
... merch
John ...
Mathew Wildgoose
Hr Ireland
Wm Bere Cooke
Jo: ...
...

Bartholomew Sheale
Refuseth to serve

A list of men from St Martin's parish serving under Captain Bowman in the City Regiment. They include a cook and a drummer and some who are listed as having a pike or a musket. There is also a note that 'Bartholomew Sheales Refuseth to serve'.

known for his Puritan and Parliamentary sympathies. These men presumably felt it safer to remain away from Oxford, though we know tantalizingly little about them. The king was under no illusions regarding their views. On 10 September 1643 he wrote to the mayor and Council:

> We understand that there are diverse aswell aldermen as Common Councell men of our Cittie of Oxford who manie monethes since have gonne from thence into rebellion or have adhered unto them, whereby that towne must needs be the worse governed, such ill members possessinge those places. We have therefore thought it necessary to recommend it to your speciall care forthwith to disfranchise and remove such as have deserved it by this their absence and . . . make choice of other able and fitt men to supply those places.

The Council searched their records (one wonders if a search was really necessary) and, agreeing that the absentees having been away during the king's stay in Oxford, would therefore seem to be 'evilly disposed' towards him, complied with the request for disfranchisement. It was, however, a reluctant submission forced on them by the presence of the king, and on 29 June 1646 almost the first action of the Council following Oxford's surrender was to repeal this act of disfranchisement, and restore all the men to their former places. In the mayoral election the following September, Alderman John Nixon was elected mayor.

Aside from the military preparations that must have made Oxford's university buildings ring with the unfamiliar sounds of anvils, smelting, forging and soldiers' drilling and marching, the king's priority was obtaining gold and silver to turn into coins to pay for the war. The colleges were asked for their treasure. Only Exeter and St John's Colleges tried to evade the requisition. In its archives Exeter College still has a small leather box containing letters that give testimony to their attempt to preserve their plate. They still have a copy of Charles' original command, signed by him personally. On 28 January 1643 they replied, explaining that they were unable to comply with his request on the grounds that it was contrary to their statutes; they even

John Nixon, who left Oxford during the war and was
replaced on the City Council at the king's request. When
Oxford surrendered in 1646 he returned and was
immediately elected mayor. (attrib. John Taylor, 1658)

quoted him the relevant part of the statute in question. The king was
clearly incensed. In a masterly reply, on the back of their own letter, he
asked them to reconsider, saying 'he did not expect, in a time when
the Commonwealth of Learning is in such danger, and Colledges
themselves not like to outlive his Majesty if he shalbe destroyed in this
Rebellion; to have found such scruples against the assisting [of] his
Majesty with what will be taken from them by those whoe endeavour
to oppress his Majesty'. Perhaps not surprisingly the college gave way,

although they asked for time to list all the plate, so that at least the donors' names could be preserved for posterity. The king gave permission for this, but requested them to be quick. The list was made and also survives today in the archives at the college. Each item handed over is described, including any inscriptions, and its weight noted. The college clearly, and rightly, had no expectation of getting anything back.

The City Council also played its part in raising money for the king's cause. As early as 10 October 1642 the Council borrowed £250 'to supply his [Charles'] present wants'. In June 1643 Charles asked the Council for a loan of ten times this amount, and again the Council felt it preferable to borrow this sum, their own coffers would seem to have been as empty as the king's. The continuing demands from the king, the lords – who met as Charles' Oxford Parliament at Christ Church in January 1644 – and the city governor became the main grievance of the townspeople. By January 1644 the Council were less compliant, refusing the lords' request for £200 per week towards the cost of the city's quarter share in the fortifications. They pointed out that their payments towards the upkeep of the regiment already stood at £120 per week. They did offer to supply labour to construct the fortifications, although even this would be difficult since 'they are much weakened in this service since the Governor's soldiers and the soldiers of the City regiment, owing to their other duties, are freed of this service'. Ten days later the governor asked for a contribution of £10 per week to pay his major to open and shut the city gates. The decision of the Council, as recorded in the Council Act Book, reflects their growing reluctance to keep up any regular payments that they felt were unnecessarily high: 'Mr Mayor desired the advice of this howse who all with one minde did say that they are unable to pay the taxes already imposed uppon them much more to pay the said weekly payment. And therefore this howse desire Mr Mayor . . . to offer him that this duty shalbe performed by some of the captaines of this Citty or by some others whom Mr Mayor and his brethren will undertake for.'

At no time are taxes popular, but the increasing demands of the Royalists fell on a city already suffering from the effects of the Civil War. Across the county 1643 was a hard year, and it was no different in Oxford. The Royalist occupation put great strains on supplies. As early as February 1643 Samuel Luke was receiving reports of shortages in Oxford: 'the King hath commanded the constables inhabiting within the 17 parishes next adjoining to Oxford to bring in straw, hay, oates, corne and all other provision whatsoever to bee imployed for his majesties service'. Samuel Brayne, one of Luke's spies or scouts had reported having to pay *2s* a night for his horse's hay while in Oxford because it was so scarce. The City Council had also taken steps to provide for lean times ahead: on 17 January they directed that wheat and maslin be procured and each of The Thirteen gave £5 towards its purchase. The grain was to be stored in the council-chamber and 'every man is desired to make as much provision for his owne family as he canne that the poore of this Cittie may have as much of this wheate and marslin as canne be spared at the rates that it is bought'. In May 1643 Luke received information that there were stores of cattle and corn being brought to Oxford 'and all the bakers imployed in making of biskett.' Later in the year there are further reports of some supplies running short: 'they have provision sufficient of all sorts and at indifferent rates, onely fewell is extreame scarce, and their beere is very ill'. From another report to Luke on 18 December 1643 it would seem that better beer was to be found elsewhere '3 or 4 troopes of horse goe dayly from Oxford to Thame, where they continue an hower or twoe drinkeing'!

The shortages were exacerbated by the huge influx of people into Oxford. The population was about ten thousand at this time and an estimated three thousand extra people arrived in the autumn and winter of 1642. At times there were probably even more. Not surprisingly, this influx, especially the increase in horse traffic, put great strain on the limited arrangements for street cleaning and public health at a time when human and animal waste was disposed of in cesspits or dungheaps behind each property, and open drains ran down the centre of the streets. In March 1643 the Council took steps to deal with the problem: 'Whereas great complaint is made to his majestie for the not cleansing the streets of this Cittie, but suffring the filth and durt to lie in the same not onelie to the scandall of the government of this place but allsoe to the great danger of breeding an infeccion amongst us'. The Council decided to nominate two men in each parish to take care of the matter, but it was a Herculean task. In August it was the king's turn to complain, he sent a writ to the mayor and bailiffs ordering the streets to be made clean. The accounts for the years 1643 and 1644 testify to the Council's efforts, there are numerous payments to unnamed men for carrying away 'loads of durt': 19*s* 4*d* for 29 loads on 24 October, £1 1*s* for 26 loads on 15 November; in the year 1642–3, 'goodman Pricket' had received £1 for cleaning the streets.

Such precautions as existed were in vain against the combined effects of overcrowding and insanitary conditions. The burial registers for the city parishes show a drastic increase in the death rate for the years 1643 and 1644. The total number of burials in 1643 was 841, as compared to 161 in 1642, 235 in 1641 and 167 in 1640. In 1644 the total had dropped to 437, but this is still double the average (see appendix). The burial registers at this time do not specify causes of death, but clearly something out of the ordinary caused this increase, and there are other sources which testify to the spread of 'plague'. Samuel Luke recorded on 7 August 1643 that 'the Queene is in Oxford & very sicke . . . they dye 20 a day of the sicknesse'. In several places in his journal he refers to 'the new disease'. Reports of the queen's sickness in early August may have been without foundation. On 22 August Luke received further information that her regiment was preparing to take her to York, 'shee being very fearefull of the new disease because a lady of honour dyed of it in the next chamber to her'. (The confusion in the reports at this time does give the impression at least of fear among the townspeople even if the actual accuracy is dubious.)

Contemporaries may have had limited understanding of disease but there were those who had an accurate idea of why the 'new disease' was so rife. Anne, Lady Fanshawe, who came to Oxford with her father recalled in her memoirs scenes of plague and sickness in Oxford, linked in her mind with overcrowded conditions. The authorities took the usual steps to prevent infection spreading unchecked, those with sickness in their houses were to remain shut up until it was over. Plague was usually worse in the summer months whereas typhus, 'the new disease' could spread at any time; in Oxford there was little relief even in winter. Less fighting was done in the winter months and Oxford quickly filled with soldiers. In December

1643 Luke recorded 'the citty is very full of soldiers . . . there are many dye dayly in Oxford of the new disease'. There is little doubt that the soldiers brought disease with them.

The burial registers also bear witness to the numbers of strangers in Oxford. Thanks to Anthony Wood's annotations in the register of St Martin's we are left with more than a mere list of names. In 1642 John Wells, described as the Earl of Sourhampton's coachman, was buried. In 1643 we get a sense of mounting chaos as the burials increase, eleven individuals are only partly named, such as 'Richard, Earl of Dorset's waggoner' and 'Mr Joseph, Head Groom of his Maties [majesties] stables'. Prince Charles, later Charles II, lost a servant in Mr Edward Poole, and the mint in New Inn Hall Street lost a master in Mr Robert Hunt. The register for St Mary Magdalen also notes soldiers and their wives and children in its pages. On 18 September 1643 a stranger was buried 'being dead in the street', and on 5 August 1644 'a stranger from the Dolphin w[hi]ch was slain'.

As with London in 1665 and 1666, the year of disease in Oxford was followed by fire. Anthony Wood left a vivid description:

> On Sunday the 8 October hapned a dreadfull fire in Oxford, such an one . . . that all ages before could hardly paralel. It began about two of the clock in the afternoon in a little poore house on the south side of Thames [George] Street . . . occasion'd by a footsoldiers roasting a pigg which he had stoln. The wind being very high & in the north, blew the flames southward very quick and strangly [strongly] & burnt all the houses & stables . . . standing between the back part of those houses that extend from the north gate to St Martin's church on the east [west side of Cornmarket St]: then all the old houses in the Bocherow [Butcher Row] . . . which stood between St Martin's church & the church of St Peter in the Baylie [Queen St], among which were two which belonged to A. Wood's mother . . . which were totally consumed.

Another (anonymous) account reported that:

> The late dreadful fire with us in Oxford began about 1 of the clock in the afternoon . . . It broke out of the North Gate called Bocardo.

The wind being fierce, it carried the Fire about the Middle of the Right Side of the Street, between the Gate & Carfax Church . . . where it fastened, . . . burning all the dwelling Houses thereabouts – back houses, Stables, with the Butcher Row. Thence in a sudden and fearful manner it razed & consumed all to Penny Farthing Street & spreading itself, burnt all St Ebbes parish . . . It may be easily judged by those that know the Town, that there can be but little less than the fourth Part of it burned down.

As might be imagined the fire left many people homeless at a time when accommodation was already at a premium. Among the City Council's complaints by October 1644 was that of 'Billetting of officers and souldiers with their wives and children [so] that roome cannot be obteyned for the poore distressed Inhabitants whose howses are burnt.'

In the light of these bitter hardships, the pressures of the Royalists' continuing financial demands exacerbated an already tense situation. Matters came to a climax on 19 October 1644. At what must have been a heated Council session, a new demand, this time from the colonel of the regiment, Sir Nicholas Selwyn, for another month's pay for the whole regiment, proved to be the last straw. The timing of the new demand could hardly have been worse. The fire had struck Oxford some ten days previously and the Council resentfully noted that Selwyn had not taken 'into his consideracon the povertye which this Citty is fallen into nor the late lamentable accident of Fire which might be a sufficient reason to cause A Charitable forbearance at the least'. The Council decided 'A Peticon Comprehending our pressures and grievances shalbe penned.'

Aside from the financial aspect of the demand, following on from an order a fortnight previously for a month's pay, it is clear that dislike of Sir Nicholas was part of the problem:

This howse doe thereupon take into consideracon that the said Sir Nicholas is a stranger to the Peticoners [that is, the Council] and was never nominated by them to his Majestie nor approved of to be their Citty Colonell, though his Majestie gave them their free choyce, Neither doth this howse conceave him to be a man that

Minutes of a meeting of the City Council, which complained about the king's demands for more money and about the behaviour of the military governor whom they considered 'only aymeth at his own ends to enrich himself by this Citty', and who had 'affronted the late mayor by assaulting and striking him'. Charles imprisoned the mayor and ordered the offending minutes to be deleted from the council book.

hath either will or power to doe this Citty any goode office but only aymeth at his owne ends and to enrich himselfe by the Citty . . . Besides he hath affronted the late Mayor [Alderman Thomas Smith] by assaulting and striking him in his place and seate in the Citty office a thing not to be forgotten by this howse!

The petition was duly written and presented by the mayor, William Chillingworth, probably accompanied by The Thirteen. It details all the payments made by the Council thus far, as well as listing other more general grievances related to the occupation and the war. The financial payments are listed as £21 per week for the Governor's pay, £5 10s for the major, towards the cost of the fortifications £2,000 plus labour, which for the last five weeks had amounted to 220 people per day. In addition the Council paid for fuel and candles for the Courts of Guard, amounting to £10 10s in summer and in autumn at least £14. Unspecified amounts were paid in excise duty and for 'Releife of common Souldiers without which it is conceaved they could not subsist.' The soldiers in the City Regiment also had to be provided for 'whose sadd condicon . . . cannot lesse then cause them to believe themselves to be the most miserable of all his Majestie's souldiers . . . their wives and familyes are distressed and themselves discontented'.

Having listed these specific 'somes, charges, and pressures' the Council declared themselves unable to meet the payments:

they must necessarilye fayle for these reasons following (vizt)
1. For that there be many of the better sort of Inhabitants lately dead and their Estates dispersed amongst their wives, children and friends.
2. For that many of the chiefest Inhabitants are gonne in to the Countrye to avoide Taxes and Straingers and Souldiers are possessed of their howses who pay little or noe Taxes.
3. That tradeing is decayed amongest the Cittizens because Forraigners [anyone from outside Oxford] being Lysted in other Regiments are mainteyned to Trade even in the Cittizens howses and doe little or noe dutyes at all, to the violacon of the Citty charters and privileges.
4. That divers Cittizens have dibursed and are engaged neare

£3000 to make up arreares of Taxes for the advance of his Majestie's service which could not be collected.

5. That by the late lamentable fire very many Inhabitants whose estates consisted of howses, howseholde Stuffe, Wares and goods, are utterly ruined, amongs which 8 common Brewhowses and 10 Bakehowses were burnt besides many malt howses, Mault, wheat, Wood and other provisions, who must be all relieved by thother Inhabitants, especially by those who are allyed and friends unto them.

The petition was duly presented on 21 October. We do not know the full details of what happened next but it is clear that the petition was not well received. On 28 October the Council Act Book records simply that 'Mr Alderman Wright, Mr Humphrey Whistler, and Mr Thomas Dennis having been imprisoned by the Lords, the Mayor and others are to present a petition, which has just been read in the house, to the Lords asking that they may be set free.' During the following week, we can only assume that negotiations took place and on 6 November the Council capitulated: 'The Act of Common Councell made the one & twentieth of October last affixed unto the Petition . . . shalbe expunged and crossed in this booke.' An order was made for the payment of a month's pay to Sir Nicholas Selwyn according to the lords' original order and a tax was to be levied at once to raise the money. The petition for the release of the imprisoned Council members was to be presented to the lords, and another tax was to be levied to raise £50 for the provision of bread for his Majesty's army.

If we look at the Council Act Book today, there is no record of the petition. The Act Book was copied up from the Minute Book, and it is in this volume that we find the petition, crossed through, but fortunately, still legible. A final, slightly defiant note was struck on 9 December: 'Mr Mayor shewed that it is desired that such charges & fees as Mr Alderman Wright Mr Whistler & Mr Dennis were inforced to pay by reason of their late imprisment should be allowed [paid for] by this Citty which this howse is well pleased to allowe in regard they suffered for this Citty.' Mr Whistler's expenses are recorded in that year's accounts as £5 12s 6d, 'allowed him when he was committed to prison about the City affairs'.

It is extremely difficult to gauge what these financial demands meant in real terms as simply converting the pounds, shillings and old pence into modern money is meaningless. There are no records of local taxation in the City Archives prior to 1666 so comparisons with the years immediately before the Civil War are difficult. However, we do have a record of the city's assessed contribution for the Ship Money tax: £100 in each year was demanded, apportioned out among the fourteen city parishes in varying amounts from £12 10s for St Mary the Virgin to £1 2s for St John's. This compares with a tax levied in December 1642, to raise £150 'for the better ordering this cittie, Universitie and countie of Oxon as well as for providing for maymed souldiers and fewell for souldiers that keepe the watches and wardes as allsoe for the buildinge of the shedds for the defence of the same souldiers from the weather'. The amounts per parish here ranged from £17 on St Aldate's and All Saints to £2 on St John's. By October 1643, when the city had to raise £1,500 for the regiment, the parishes were paying amounts from £170 (St Mary the Virgin, All Saints and St Martin's) to £18 (St John's). In addition, at this time they were paying weekly amounts of between 12s and £8 16s for the defences, and a further tax of between £10 and £105 to raise £1,095 for the governor's pay. This is at a time when wages were usually only a few shillings a week. The Council took some action to limit the demands made on the citizens for taxes. As already described, money was borrowed or the wealthier members of the Common Council contributed comparatively large sums themselves. On the king's arrival in Oxford following the Battle of Edgehill he was presented with £520 raised from such contributions. The mayor gave £50 and others £10, Humphrey Whistler gave £5, William Chillingworth (a future mayor) gave £4. The fact that these men found such sums gives an indication of their wealth, and perhaps puts the parish taxation into perspective. The poorer people did not pay, it would have needed only a few wealthier tradespeople in each parish to raise the bulk of the money. The problem of the 'burden of taxation' that the Council were to complain about may have had its roots in the fact that people were unable to recoup the losses they had suffered because of the effect of the war on trade. The Council also derived much of its income from rents derived from leasehold properties. There are indications in the City Archives that these were difficult to collect, in the year 1643–4 an allowance of £13 15*s* was made for 'Rents forborne for a time by reason of these distracted times but to be collected as speedy as may be.' The following year the allowance for unpaid rents had risen to £42 18*s* 11*d*.

As well as money, the Council was responsible for another important contribution, the hay crop from Port Meadow. An agreement for this to be given to Charles for his cavalry was made annually during the occupation. Each year the king made a new request, which was agreed to by the Council. In March 1644 it was a little grudging: 'It is unanimously consented unto that his majesty shall have the first cropp of the said Meadow this present ensuing yeare Provided that . . . the cittizens be not compelled to helpe make the hay therof or to make any allowance of money towards the makeing thereof.' The following spring another politely worded request from the king was again granted, though it was reiterated that the citizens were to have use of the meadow after the king had taken the first crop.

One aspect of the pressures the town found itself under was the worsening of the always tense relations between the Council and the university. The university was very much independent of the Council, those who traded with the colleges lay outside the Council's usual control over trade and those who practised particular trades or professions. Members of the university were exempt from Council imposed taxes and it was this that caused the problems. The City Council and the university were each jealous of their own rights and privileges, and were quick to react to perceived extensions of the other's powers. When Charles and his court first arrived in Oxford, he does not seem to have taken this fact fully into account. His own pressing need for money may have made him somewhat careless as to who provided it, or how exactly it was raised!

In June 1643 the king asked the Council to raise £2,000 'by taxation or otherwise amongst all the inhabitants of this Cittie and suburbs thereof . . . aswell priviledge as others'. Charles went on 'our will and pleasure is that all priviledges and orders to the contrarie shall be sett aside; soe as noe head of anie Colledge or hall or anie schollar therein resideinge be taxed'. (i.e., the privilege as to not being taxed may be set aside.)

Given the historic struggle between town and gown, The Thirteen must have fallen on this royal dispensation with glee. Not surprisingly the university protested. They presented a petition, asking that their ancient privileges, as granted by Charles' predecessors in their charters, be preserved, in particular, the privilege that members of the university may not be taxed by the townsmen. They requested that the vice-chancellor assess the share of the new taxation that should be born by the privileged persons. It is not difficult to imagine the king's exasperation with what must have seemed to him, in the light of his own position, a trivial dispute. We can only assume that he realized the unwisdom of offending the university. In July he confirmed their rights and privileges and appointed three of his retinue, including the Earl of Bristol, to decide how the money should be raised.

The Council were not easily persuaded, however, and presented their own petition. They pointed out that they had assessed the £2,000 as commanded and that they had not in fact included any of the scholars in the assessment. They admitted to having assessed some of the privileged persons, but only those who lived within Oxford itself. They also complained that the university was extending its privileges 'to all sorts of people viz. esquires, counsellors at law, attorneys, bakers, brewers, apothecaries, inneholders, carriers, tailors, barbers, ironmongers, carpenters, slatters, joyners, masons and other mechannick trades, alehousekeepers, women and reteyners, whereas few of them be their meniall servants, as they ought to be'. They claimed these people numbered 221. About £1,600 had been collected. They asked for their own nominated representatives to join the three lords already named to settle the dispute.

The matter was resolved on 15 August. The university had assessed its own contribution to the £2,000 as only £40. In a spirit of compromise, both sides agreed to submit to the lords' ruling as to the raising of the rest. The lords decided that the mayor and the vice-chancellor should meet to decide this, on the understanding that the solution would not prejudice the privileges of either side (and therefore could not be seen as setting a precedent). The lords and the king then washed their hands on what they must have seen as a tiresome affair. It is not clear from the records what the final settlement was.

This was by no means the only dispute between the Council and the university during this time, and it serves as an example of how, even in the middle of the Civil War, people were often more taken up with their own concerns than with those of the king and Parliament.

One aspect of occupied Oxford which seems to have united all sides was the unpopularity of the military governors, of whom the most infamous was Sir Arthur Aston. Even Anthony Wood – notable for his support of all things Royalist – admitted Aston was 'a testy, froward, imperious and tirannical person, hated in Oxon and elswhere by God and man'. Prior to his appointment at Oxford, Aston was governor in Reading, and Samuel Luke reports his cruelty there as well. In February 1643 some of the inhabitants of Reading were imprisoned for non-payment of taxes and for 'those men that are gone they imprison their wives in their stead'. Later the same month 140 of the prisoners taken at Cirencester were sent to Aston in Reading, who promptly sent them back to Oxford, 'they making miserable complaints for bread and other necessaries in their journey, which make the contrye stand much in feare of him [Aston]'. Even allowing for Luke exaggerating, we can understand that Oxford may well have been dismayed when Aston was put in command.

One night in December 1643 Aston was assaulted, though the details are difficult to establish. Luke's initial information was that: 'on Thursday night last the governor of Oxford was rideing in the streets, his footman runing by him who josseled a gentleman. The governor bid his footman cut the gentleman. Then the gentleman strucke the teeth out of his [the footman's] head and ran a tilt at the governor and ran his sword against one of his rib[s] . . . its likely to prove mortall which the generallity of the city pray for.' Two days later, on 26 December, he added 'the governor of Oxford was stabbed the last weeke, which all the citty is extreme glad of'. Sadly for Oxford Aston recovered from his wound and in spite of an optimistic rumour that he was to be replaced, he continued as governor 'dayly attended by a guard consisting of 4 men in long redd coates and halberds'. Aston was finally replaced in December 1644 by Colonel Legge, as the result of a further incident which must have amused the citizens as it clearly amused Anthony Wood. In September 1644 Aston was 'kervetting on horsback in Bullington green before certaine ladies, his horse flung him and broke his legge: so that being cut off and he therupon rendred useless for employment, one coll. Legge succeeded him. Soone after the country people comming to the market would be ever and anon asking the sentinell "who was governor of Oxon?" They answered "one Legge." Then replied they:– "A pox upon him! Is he governour still?".

There is one final, rather grisly anecdote about Aston, despite being 'rendred useless for employment' his part in the Civil War was not played out until 1649. He was Governor of Drogheda in Ireland when the town was stormed by Cromwell and his troops in September of that year. In the massacre that followed, Aston was beaten to death with his own wooden leg.

Anthony Wood's more humorous tale about Aston serves as a reminder that there was a lighter side to life even in the middle of the Civil War. In spite of the hardships, Oxford must have been an exciting place to be in. The king had visited the town earlier in his reign, but now he and his court took up residence. In a world without modern media and communications it was a rare treat for ordinary people to come into such close proximity with their royal family. The king and, later, Henrietta Maria were welcomed by university and Council in traditional style, and whatever the private misgivings of some, the pageantry and ceremony were an excuse for celebrations. Indeed, given the timing of the queen's arrival, July 1643, it must have been a relief to be able to celebrate. In the weeks prior to her arrival, even Luke recorded that 'much preparation for her entertaynment' was being made. Anthony Wood, however, was critical of the apparent lack of enthusiasm shown by the Council:

> on Friday in the eveninge the kinge and queene, with all their traine, came into Oxford. They rode into Christchurch in a coach . . . there was a speech made to the queene for her entertainement & wellcome; bookes of verses & gloves presented to her by the Universitie. Mr Dennys, the mayor of the towne, accompanied only with his mace bearer on horse backe, brought his majestie into Christ–church, the mayor in scarlett bearinge the mace uppon his owne shoulder, ridinge with Garter the cheife of the heraldes . . . but no other of the towne came with him.

This account may be sour grapes on Wood's part, the Council had discussed the matter on 13 July (the day before she arrived) and certainly intended to greet the queen with all ceremony in the usual fashion at Penniless Bench 'in their best aray and there stande readie against her Majesties comeinge' and the mayor was directed to choose a suitable gift. Looking at the accounts this was probably also traditional: £5 was allowed for a pair of gloves presented to her majesty. The accounts also record expenses of £3 8s 2d for wine and 6s 6d for strewing flowers on the day of her arrival.

In addition to these celebrations, bonfires were lit and church bells rung whenever there was news of a military victory. Wood makes frequent references to this and Luke recorded on 27 March 1644 that Charles had received good news from Rupert about the siege of Newark; 'the king was so joyfull at the news that he presently knighted the messenger and caused the letter to be printed and the bells to bee rung and bonfires to bee made in Oxford untill 12 of the klock in the night'.

The presence of the king meant that the business of the court was conducted in Oxford, and this included entertaining. The French Ambassador visited Charles there in October 1643. He was conducted in state to Christ Church – another notable person and another show for the townspeople to look at – and was present at a banquet the same evening. On 24 November 1643 Luke was told that 'The King, Queene & Prince Rupert were invited to supper upon Wedsonday night and for the most part of the night they was danceing, they was likewise invited to supper at another colledge upon Thursday last.' Luke's tone seems slightly disapproving of such gaiety, but such events gave Oxford people plenty to talk about.

In January 1644 preparations began for the Oxford Parliament. The spread of printed news-sheets must have meant that many of the members were household names, and again their arrival provided food for the curious.

Of a less happy nature were the sights afforded by the war: prisoners, soldiers, executions of spies, enemy soldiers or deserters. Wood recorded on 18 March 1643 the hanging of a Parliamentary soldier 'uppon the gibbet standinge at Carfox conduit, for killing of a woaman dwellinge about Gloster-hall'. Crowds would gather to watch such events, and also to jeer at the prisoners as they made their way to the castle.

Taken on balance the years 1642–4 were difficult for Oxford people as for those elsewhere. They had endured high taxes and food shortages, had their homes taken over by soldiers and their livelihoods disrupted. Many suffered from disease, losing loved ones, friends and neighbours. The fire destroyed a sizeable proportion of the town and plunged many into even greater poverty. There seems from Luke's reports and even Wood, to have been a sense of war weariness. In 1645 and 1646 the war would come closer still to Oxford as the city found itself the object of enemy ambition when first Essex and then Fairfax turned their attention to destroying 'the Mother Seat to hold up the spirit of the Enemy'.

CHAPTER 5

'FROM CIVIL WAR GOOD LORD DELIVER US'

This prayer, inscribed on the new bridge at Cropredy in the 1930s, appears to have been answered in mainland Britain, where we have managed to live more or less at peace with each other, at least without further open warfare, since the seventeenth century. Ireland has been the obvious exception to this, and experience there and elsewhere in Europe even in the present century, is a reminder of the special horror of war between people who are close neighbours. All war is terrible and inevitably causes attrocities: civil war appears worse because it seems more unnatural. The English Civil War was no exception and brought its full share of suffering to people in all parts of the country. Those in Oxfordshire were subjected to none of the major battles and only one minor one, but there was a succession of raids and skirmishes, and it had more than its share of the suffering and unpleasantness that came from continual occupation by a hostile military force – hostile not necessarily in terms of political allegiance (though this was true for some), but in its attitude towards resentful civilians. For Oxfordshire people it very soon became clear that it made little difference which side you were on when undisciplined soldiers needed food and lodging, or anything else that took their fancy.

It used to be thought that life went on pretty much as normal away from the main battlefields, but historians now know that this was not the case. Much of the evidence has only recently come to light. Shortly before the inscription was put up on Cropredy Bridge it was possible for a reputable Oxford historian to write of Great Rollright: 'The battle of Edgehill took place too far off to have much interest for the people of this village . . . The first actual sight that the villagers had of the armies was on 2 September 1643, when Essex marched along the main road from Banbury to Chipping Norton, leaving the village one and a half miles to the north-west.' The picture thus presented is now known to be far from the true experience even of quite small and remote villages. It implies that there was no action to disrupt people's daily lives except when battles were fought close by or armies marched along the roads through the middle of the village. Armies did not in fact march along main roads in the neat and orderly sense suggested by such descriptions. Seventeenth-century roads were unmetalled and frequently unfenced, passing through a largely unenclosed countryside of arable fields. When the surface became churned up or the potholes too deep, travellers found a way around them, often encroaching on the edges of neighbouring fields. The lumbering wagons of an army's baggage train, its artillery dragged by teams of cart-horses, and as many of the soldiers as possible no doubt tried to use the roads, but would often have found the surface worse than less-trampled areas of open fields and commons. In any case, an army could not march in a single long column along the line of a road, but was forced to spread out over the countryside simply in order to forage for supplies, so that it must have covered a front several miles wide. Individual regiments and troops made their own way as best they could to the next rendezvous. The mile and a half distance from the main road would certainly not have protected Great Rollright from the unwelcome attention of Essex's soldiers. Earlier on that very march he had himself deplored the fact that 'being forced when we move to march with the whole army, which can be but slowly . . . the counties must suffer much wrong, and the cries of the poor people are infinite'.

Rather surprisingly, however, few parish records have much to say about this widespread situation. Recent research concentrating mainly on south Warwickshire and parts of the north of Oxfordshire has highlighted the claims made by individual parishes for compensation for damage and loss suffered by their inhabitants during the war. Such claims were made to Parliament after the war and reveal the detail of financial hardships suffered by local people whose meagre food supplies were eaten up without payment, their crops trampled and their horses and wagons requisitioned, quite apart from the physical abuse and terror they may have been subjected to. On the other hand, records like parish registers and the annual accounts presented to the parish meetings by churchwardens, often say very little explicitly about the war. At Witney, a town certainly not unaffected by the war, the churchwardens' accounts continued routinely year after year with no unusual items, and the inventory of church goods continued to list the same mundane items including 'four scaffold poles, two brazen pulleys and a length of timber', presumably needed when work was required to the church roof, but, one imagines, equally useful to any passing army anxious to construct siege towers or simply to repair its carts and other equipment. Civic affairs appear to have continued in Abingdon according to references in the borough records. Cakes, sugar, beer and wine were provided for the judges holding the assize court there, and the town's officials continued to collect rents and dole out charities. There is other evidence elsewhere in the records to show that life was

The lopsided appearance of the nave in Radley church is the result of fighting there when Cavaliers occupied it and were attacked by Roundhead troops. The north side of the church was destroyed.

often far from normal in Abingdon, a key garrison for first Royalists and then Parliamentarians. It is often a matter of 'reading between the lines' and noticing what the parish records do not say. The churchwardens at Oddington on Otmoor bought a new book for their accounts in 1609 and carefully inscribed the first page like a schoolchild with a new exercise book, and successive holders of the office kept meticulous records of income and expenditure each year. They become notably sparse in detail between 1643 and 1646 and then stop altogether until 1649. One of the last entries notes that for the year 1644–5 income was seriously reduced, there being no rates collected for several properties. Almost certainly this is an indication of the problems that beset many families, especially on the disputed eastern side of the county where the frontier shifted back and forth and raiding parties from one side or the other were never far away. Another clue to the situation may lie in Oddington's annual list of church goods which, up to Easter 1643, includes 'a silver chalice with cover of silver', but when the accounts resume after the war both these items are missing. Were they some plundering soldier's loot?

The presence of the king at Oxford meant that the whole county became occupied territory. An outer ring of defences was created to keep the enemy at bay, and to secure the whole of the wealth and resources of the region for the support of the Royalist army and court at Oxford. Everything from horses, carts and wagons, wheat, butter, cloth and leather to timber and scrap metal was desperately needed to keep the army in the field, and above all manpower and money were required in large amounts. The Parliamentary armies had the same needs, and those places unfortunate enough to be on the borders of Oxfordshire were likely to be taxed and plundered by both sides. Major strongholds like Banbury Castle in the north and Wallingford, Abingdon and Donnington Castle near Newbury to the south guarded the main supply lines to Oxford and at the same time threatened communications between Parliamentary London and the western side of the country. Every market town had its garrison and manor-houses up and down the county were strengthened with moats and earthworks and any other fortifications their owners could devise. Faringdon House was strengthened to protect the western approach and Gaunt House guarded the key crossing of the Thames above the city at Newbridge near Standlake. To the north of Oxford, Woodstock Manor, the old royal hunting lodge, was surrounded by earthworks, and on the vulnerable eastern frontier Bletchingdon, Boarstall, Brill, Shirburn and Greenland House formed a chain of fortified outposts. Parliament too had its local strongholds. From the spring of 1643 it held Henley, and here one of Whitelock's houses, Phyllis Court, was protected with earthworks and gun emplacements as a counterbalance to the Royalist Greenland House a little distance away. The owners of these houses defended them with their servants, tenants and small detachments of soldiers, while larger garrisons were based in the more important towns. Wallingford had a garrison of one thousand under the energetic Colonel Blagge.

The role of these garrisons was not purely defensive, and raiding parties ranged far and wide harassing the enemy and engaging in their favourite game of 'beating up quarters'. This usually meant a troop of fast-moving light horsemen descending on a village in the early hours of the morning hoping to catch enemy soldiers sleeping in their billets and killing or capturing as many as possible. It is surprising how far afield such parties were able to roam, especially from the larger garrison towns. Oddington near Stow-on-the-Wold was attacked by a party from Gloucester in June 1643, and Prince Rupert's celebrated raid on Chinnor, which led to the skirmish at Chalgrove Field, was an example of the same technique carried out from Oxford. Thame changed hands several times, being held first by one side and then the other and was repeatedly subjected to raiding parties from both. Anthony Wood, who ironically had been sent there for greater safety, wrote of the 'great disturbances and affrightments' suffered by the vicar's household where he and his brother lodged. These came from the soldiers 'of both parties'. He gives a graphic description in which one can sense both the fear and the excitement of the occasion when a party of Blagge's troops were being hotly chased back to Wallingford by superior numbers of Parliamentarians they had encountered on one of their raids near Crendon:

After the action was concluded at Crendon, and Blagge and his men forced to fly homeward, they took part of Thame in their way. [Anthony Wood] and his fellow sojourners being all then at dinner in the parlour . . . they were all alarumed with their approach: and by that time they could run out of the house into the backside to look over the pale that parts it from the common road, they saw a great number of horsemen posting towards Thame from Crendon Bridge about a stone's cast from their house . . . and in the head of them was Blagge with a bloody face, and his party with Captain Walter's following him. The number as was then guessed by A.W. and those of the family was 50 or more, and they all rode under the said pale and close to the house. They did not ride in order but each made shift to be foremost. And one of them riding upon a shelving ground opposite to the dore, his horse slip'd, fell upon one side, and threw the rider (a lusty man) in A. Wood's sight. Colonel Crafford who was well horsed and at a pretty distance before his men in pursuite, held a pistol to him; but the trooper crying 'quarter' the rebells came up, rifled him and took him and his horse away with them. Crafford rode on without touching him, and ever or anon he would be discharging his pistol at some of the fag-end of Blagge's horse who rode through the west end of Thame.

It was all terribly exciting to be a spectator of such events, but very different to get caught up in the action as must often have happened. After this same raid it was reported that the people of Long Crendon planned to protect themselves in future by ringing the church bells in an upward peal as a signal which would bring local men and perhaps troops in to their defence. As Rupert left Chinnor after his succesful raid in June 1643 someone set fire to the thatch of the houses so that several villagers were left homeless. Then there were the many occasions when soldiers from a nearby garrison came looking for food, supplies and money for their own use. Such garrisons were expected to support themselves, and the normal way to do this was to buy what it had money to pay for and to obtain the rest by threats or violence. Each garrison commander was a law to himself. While the king or Essex might both deplore the suffering inflicted on innocent country people and issue decrees and official lists of fair prices to be given for goods, garrison commanders and individual soldiers were able to ignore them. Among the worst was the Roundhead Colonel Purefoy based at the Earl of Northampton's captured house at Compton

Wynyates, who terrorized a large area of south Warwickshire and north Oxfordshire. Almost as bad was the situation around Banbury where the Earl of Northampton himself commanded a garrison which Parliamentarians referred to as 'That Den of Theeves'. His subordinate and agent colonel Gerard Croker of Hook Norton, who seems to have been well in favour with the king and Rupert, was so harsh on the local inhabitants in demanding contributions that the Earl himself complained. Both Blagge at Wallingford and Brown at Abingdon ranged widely over the countryside around those places, seizing supplies for themselves and intercepting those of the enemy. When things were hard at Wallingford because there was no money to pay the garrison and their meat supply had gone rotten, Blagge sent his men out to pillage the surrounding villages for whatever they could get. According to one of Luke's informants, 'They search the country for bacon and take it away and carry it into the castle. The soldiers have no pay but are permitted to fetch cattle out of the contry instead of their pay.' There could be little peace or safety for the inhabitants of villages within reach of such garrisons.

Apart from their own needs, the garrison towns were responsible for ensuring that Oxfordshire's contribution to the support of the field army based there was collected and sent to Oxford. As for Ship Money or any other tax, the county's total was divided between the towns and villages according to their supposed ability to pay, but the amount of the assessment in this case far exceeded anything they had been asked for before. In 1643 the levy for the county was £1,176 every week – over £61,000 for the year, which was more than seventeen times greater than the Ship Money levy of 1635. The greatest share of this fell on Ploughley, Wootton, Chadlington and Bampton Hundreds, each of which had to find £147 per week. ('Hundreds' were ancient administrative districts into which a county was divided.) Banbury and Bloxham Hundreds got off with half that amount, while the town of Henley was assessed at £15, though it is unlikely that much of this was collected as Henley was taken over by Parliamentary forces early in 1643 and held by them for the rest of the war. This would only mean, however, that a contribution would be demanded from the other side. The assessments for the remaining hundreds were: Bullingdon £100, Ewelme £80, Lewknor £50,

Thame and Pyrton £42 each, Binfield £39, and Langtree £35. Considerable persuasion would be required to extract such weekly amounts and soldiers were used to put pressure on reluctant parish constables, or simply to apply direct force to recalcitrant individual payers. A document survives which was issued in 1644 in connection with the levy of £1,200 a week for that year. It refers to it as a 'weekly loan to His Majesty's horse in the county', and sets out in precise bureaucratic detail the division of responsibility for collection between the petty constables and the local military commander, an appeals procedure, and arrangements for compensation should the soldiers happen to take more than the regulations permitted when distraining the goods of those refusing to pay. All this suggests a well-regulated administrative system, fair to both sides, such as might have operated in an ideal peacetime situation, but is almost impossible to believe in the context of civil war. Not for the last time, senior management was completely out of touch with the reality of the situation on the ground.

Towards the end of the same document the desire is expressed 'That His Majesty's Horse be quartered if it may be, in Market Townes, and Townes of Thorough-fare, where are conveniency of stabling and Victualing houses, as places most convenient, and for the more ease of the farmer leaving convenient stabling and lodgeing in inns for entertainment of Travellers.' The ease of farmers and entertainment of travellers were not the priorities uppermost in the minds of garrison commanders or their hardened troops. Such a document was hardly likely to have much effect on actual conditions, and those who saw it nailed up in the parish church must have smiled wryly. They sent petitions to the king complaining about the heavy burden of taxation which was ruining them, and the impossibility of finding the money since their means of making a livelihood were being disrupted by marauding soldiers, the requisitioning of horses and wagons, damage to crops and restrictions on trade. Among the casualties of war were the locks which had taken so many years to construct making the Thames navigable up to Oxford. They were destroyed in 1644 after Abingdon had fallen into enemy hands. Merchants were suffering particularly from the ban on trade with London, from which much of their wealth was derived. In spite of Parliament having imposed a similar ban at its end on trade with

Oxford, profit was a greater incentive than principal for some and ways of getting round the ban were found at least in the early part of the war. Luke was informed by one of his spies that carriers were bringing wagon-loads of goods out of the capital, telling the guards on the road that they were for the use of the Parliamentary garrison at Wycombe to whom they were ostentatiously addressed, but they were then diverted to Oxford where the Cavaliers were pleased to pay for them.

As in all wars some people doubtless managed to make profit. Anthony Wood sourly accused the merchants and tradesmen of Oxford of growing fat on the profits of supplying the court, and there must have been innumerable occasions when opportunities for extra paid work arose even in small villages. Searching for evidence of death and destruction in the pages of churchwardens' account books, one frequently finds entries recording the payment of money to local people for all manner of tasks which were increased because of the war. Bell-ringers did particularly well in Burford: 'Payed the ringers when the kinge came first to Burford, 5s 0d,' and then 'Payed more to the ringers for the kinge, 8s 0d' and 'Payed the ringers for the Prince, 2s 0d.' One senses that the ringers were onto a good thing, and it may have been their enthusiasm for the task or pure patriotic zeal which led to the bells needing to be repaired after all this extra ringing – and of course another local tradesman being paid for the work: 'Payed for mending the bell wheeles, 1s 0d' and again 'Payed for mending the wheeles another tyme, 2s 0d.'

All over the county skilled men like blacksmiths, farriers and wheelwrights were in great demand and, if they were paid for their work, must have done very well. Charles I's 'Sergeant Painter', William Dobson, was another who experienced a huge increase in demand for his talents, and a stream of courtiers and officers came to have their portraits painted by him. Because his customers tended to be here today and gone tomorrow, he devised the practice of asking for 50 per cent of the money up front. In spite of his business acumen he died heavily in debt after the war.

Official taxation was bad enough, unofficial plundering was much worse. Plunder of the enemy's goods was fair game. The Wiltshire clothiers who formed themselves into a large convoy of pack animals

and tried to buy immunity by paying large sums to Royalist garrisons
on their way to London, were stopped by a party of Blagge's troopers
and herded into Wallingford. This was not the first time the long-
suffering Wiltshire clothiers had been plundered as it was reported in
June 1643 that 'there are a great many soldiers come from Wallingford
to Oxford to have new clothes made with the cloth which they tooke
from the Wiltshire carryers . . . they say they have taken so much cloth
from the Roundheads as will make new clothes for all their soldiers'.
Cloth to make uniforms was a very important commodity to an army
in the field, as were boots and shoes. After any battle the bodies of the
dead, and often the wounded as well, were stripped and their clothing
taken as prizes of war. Cloth from the Cotswolds was just as important
to the king as iron from the Forest of Dean when he set out to secure
Cirencester and Gloucester.

Pillaging could also be used as a form of punishment for those
known to sympathize with the enemy, and the practice was used by
both sides. It could be used against individuals or whole communities.
In January 1645 a troop of Cavaliers came to Chipping Norton where
they found billets for the night, but before leaving next morning they
looted every house in the town, taking £40 from one man and driving
off 200 sheep and other livestock. We do not know what had
prompted this outrage. Chipping Norton lay within Royalist territory
but like many north Oxfordshire towns it included many Puritans and
Parliamentary sympathizers. The best known case of pillaging a
private house in the county is that of Byron's troops wrecking
Bulstrode Whitelock's Fawley Court in 1642. This is Whitelock's own
description of it:

> 1000 of them being in and about his house, there was no insolence
> or outrage which such guests commit upon an enemy but these
> brutish soldiers did it at Fawley Court. There they had their whores,
> they spent and consumed in one night 100 loads of corn and hay,
> littered their horses with good wheat sheaves, gave them all sorts of
> corn in the straw, made great fires in the closes, and William Cook
> telling them there were billetts and faggots nearer to them than the
> plough timber which they burned, they threatened to burn him . . .
> Whatsoever they could lay their hands on they carried away or

spoiled, and did all that malice and rapine could provoke barbarous mercenaries to commit.

Whitelock, as a leading supporter of Parliament, was an obvious target for Royalist soldiers for his politics as well as his wealth. Byron apparently ordered them not to harm his belongings, but even if this is true the order was ignored. Perhaps even more galling for Whitelock was the damage to two other properties he owned in Henley by soldiers of his own side who formed the garrison there. The Bell Inn was set on fire 'as some supposed by the carelessness of some Parliament soldiers quartered there', and his bitter comment on the damage done at his other main house, Phyllis Court, was that 'bruitish soldiers make no distinctions' between friend and foe when it came to wrecking property. The garrison stationed in Phyllis Court illustrates the worst features of the behaviour of such soldiers: apart from damaging the house they mutinied against their governor and threatened to kill him. Major General Brown was sent in to restore order on this occasion, but complaints multiplied because the men of

The defences of Phyllis Court, Henley. This curious painting was copied from the original found on the plaster behind some panelling when the old house was being rebuilt. The uniforms are of early eighteenth-century style, suggesting that the original painting was not done until long after the Civil War. It apparently shows the moat, ramparts and drawbridge constructed to turn this house into a fortified stronghold for Parliament.

the garrison were plundering the townspeople, and they were only finally disciplined by the imposition of martial law with its summary justice and severe penalties, imposed on them with the agreement of Parliament.

The complaints of the townspeople of Henley must have been echoed in every other town in Oxfordshire which had to put up with the presence of troops – the drunken brawls, intimidation and stealing, harassment of women, increased dirt and disease and the general unpleasantness caused by unruly soldiers in wartime. Oxford, being the largest town and the king's capital, suffered most, but other towns and even much smaller villages had their own experience of this side of the war. It was worst for those who actually had soldiers billeted in their homes, either as part of a permanent garrison or as a regiment passing through, which could descend like a hoard of locusts on already impoverished and frightened villagers. Sergeant Henry Foster fought with the London Trained Bands and wrote the following:

> Thurs 31 August wee advanced from thence to a village called Stretton Ardley; this night our brigade consisting of six regiments . . . were all quartered at this little village. It is conceived we were in all this brigade about five thousand. Here was little provision either for officers or souldiers. The night before we came hither the cavaliers were at Bister two miles from this village.

Foster is complaining about the suffering of the troops, but what about the villagers, occupied for the second time in two nights by rival armies? (Stratton Audley probably had a population of two or three hundred people on whom the five thousand descended.) The task of the quartermaster was to find lodging for his men and he would go first to all the local inns and lodging houses, but when they were full, private households were ordered to provide accommodation for the remainder. The large houses of wealthy men, especially those considered 'delinquents', were made to take large numbers, as billeting was always seen as a means of punishing such men, but the cottages of ordinary folk were no doubt used as well and the rest would sleep in barns and outbuildings or in the open.

Billets were supposed to be paid for at set rates which were published: 8*d* per day for troopers, 7*d* for dragoons and 6*d* for foot-soldiers, but very often there was no money available or forthcoming and 'tickets' were issued instead which were supposed to be redeemable for cash at a later date. Any reluctance to accept the soldiers was seen as opposition to the king's (or Parliament's) cause and would only make things worse.

The Revd Thomas Wyatt was probably willing enough to help the king's cause by 'entertaining' soldiers in Ducklington rectory, but both the cost and their behaviour made him nervous and he lost some small personal belongings: 'When the king went from Oxford above 60 soldiers at one time and as many more another were lodged att howses, above 20 more and horses entertained at the parsonage. Spent in victalls and fodder and corn worth £5. One sargeant major Daniol and Mr Kingsmore lodged in my chamber with a great charge of money and precious thinges. They did no hurt but some or other took away my glasse and comb.' One senses that the rector felt a tingle of excitement at being part of these events, but

The Old Rectory, Ducklington, where the Revd Thomas Wyatt wrote his journal recording the soldiers billeted in his house and other excitements of the war.

he was rather shocked by the next visitation: 'The same day Captain Snead came to see me in his passage to Faringdon, a goodly gentleman but very drunke, did swear most fearfully and took some horses.' Wyatt clearly took an interest in the men who stayed with him, often noting the places they came from: 'August 19 1643 billetted at my house a Coronet called Locket of Staffordshire and a quarter master called Littlefear of Nottingham and Pierce of Newport with 3 men and 7 horses of Sir John Byron['s] regiment and under Captain Meynils company under Sir Charles Lucas . . . There was with them one Winget a Leicestershire man that carried the colours a stammering fellow . . . one was a smith and farrier . . . a mad merry fellow.'

As the war went on the note of cheerfulness went out of his journal, especially in 1644 and 1645 when parliamentary troops appeared in Ducklington, with whom he clearly had a very different relationship. They had little respect for the seventy-year-old rector, taking away several of his horses including his old black mare and a cart which was used by the constable to carry provisions. (Was this a case of collaboration, the Witney area having many Parliamentary supporters, or was the constable simple acting under duress from the troops?) Worst of all, 'These parliament soldiers took away the surplice . . . pulled down a little crosse [and] tore the communion book to the psalms.' He suffered some pretty hostile billeting the following year when on 'March 16 1645 I had a ticket to billet 80 soldiers, the men of parliament, the most unreasonable that ever we had. Went away 18 of March in the morning. Spent about £20 and spoiled any thing. These came again March 24 and baited and supped and breakfasted and spent and spoiled as much as was possible in so short a space.' The cruellest act of all was that his son Henry, aged twenty-two, was taken prisoner 'in my stead' by soldiers who came in the night. Perhaps he had said or done something to annoy them, but he would probably be made to pay a large sum for his freedom.

A few rash words spoken in the heat of the moment could bring severe retribution. James Carey reported to Samuel Luke in August 1643 'that there were about 30 of the king's forces yesterday at Thame & took away all the horses they could find and pillaged one man's howse because when some of the prisoners which were taken on the king's side at Chinner were brought thither hee wished them all hanged & Prince Rupert also'. A particularly chilling threat was issued by Henry Wilmot (later Lord Wilmot of Adderbury) to prevent the men of Adderbury again going to the aid of John Fiennes in Banbury when the Earl of Northampton was trying to seize his six cannon in the summer of 1642. He had a lot of trouble from the strong Parliament faction in the village, but on this occasion his threat to 'string up the men and send the soldiers to their wives and children' was well understood and totally effective.

Personal violence inevitably occurred between soldiers and civilians, but the scanty references rarely record the circumstances. Hannah Roads was buried in Banbury in July 1645, 'Executed by the soldiars that held the castel for the king', while a year earlier a soldier was 'slain pulling down Humphry Robbin's housewall', which suggests that the killing was not all one way. In Bicester an unnamed 'stranger slain by a souldyer', in Great Rollright 'William Sheppard Esq. slaine by one of the King's souldiers' and in Shipton-under-Wychwood 'Thos. Rawlins slain by one of the King's soldiers' were all buried in 1644. The registers also record the deaths of soldiers killed by their fellow soldiers. These may have been unfortunate accidents or may have resulted from brawls like the one in Oxford in 1642 or more personal disputes between individuals. There was obviously some sort of trouble in Burford during November 1644 when Thomas Williams, a trooper, 'was slaine by his fellow soldier with shott of pistoll', and a week later Lewis Davies 'a serjeant of a foote company under Gen. Gerrard dyed of a wound given him by a captaine'. Sometimes there were particularly brutal incidents like the hanging of a Royalist soldier in Thame described in *Mercurius Rusticus*, a Royalist newsheet. His Roundhead tormentors took great delight in stringing him up from the swinging sign of the King's Head Inn. As with most hangings, death was not immediate. Victims were usually put out of their agony by friends who pulled down on the body to speed strangulation, but in this case we are told that a cruel Roundhead soldier lifted the man's legs to make him suffer longer, twisting him round to face the picture of his king on the painted inn sign, to the amusement of some of the onlookers.

Hanging was the normal sentence for spies if they were caught, but it seems that few were. In a civil war where friend and foe were difficult to distinguish, spies could mingle easily with local people without attracting suspicion. They were certainly used by both sides and while it is difficult to be sure how useful their information was to their commanders, it is a very revealing source to later historians. Sir Samuel Luke, one of the officers in Essex's army who fought at Chalgrove with Hampden and was later governor of Newport Pagnell, was appointed Scout-master General to Essex. Part of his journal has survived and shows that numerous spies were going out every few days to different Royalist towns and bringing back information, which Luke carefully recorded. Most of it concerned enemy troop movements but sometimes it was about morale in the king's army or garrisons. The following entry for 12 July 1643 is typical:

> Robert Cox went this day; Mr Paul Luke went forth alsoe. Ralph Norton returned this day and saith that the King with about 2000 horse and 3 regiments of foote lyes still in and about Woodstocke and as [he] heares they have 25 peeces of ordnance and that he is expected to come to Banbury, and that quarters were taken upp the last night for him att Deddington but hee came not. That there were 30 carts of maymed soldiers came on Monday last into Oxford from Prince Maurice out of the west. That some of the King's horse should have quartered at Bister but the plague being there prevented them.

One can sense the shocked tones of Puritan disapproval in which the following report of goings-on at the Cavalier court in Oxford was read: 'that he saw Prince Rupert and a lady in a coach together whoe went into the court with him, and that she had a round black velvet cap on, and a long white feather with a redd tipp at the end of it. And that she went in with her arme akimboe, like a commander.'

Sometimes spies were stopped and questioned, but as often as not they seem to have evaded discovery. Robert Cox told how he and Ralph Norton had been taken by some of the king' troopers who seemed more interested in robbing them of their money than anything else, and having done so, released them again. Henry Hopkins was stopped and questioned at Wheatley Bridge and kept in custody all night, but in the morning he too was released. One of the difficulties in identifying spies was that they were probably local men who could easily explain their presence or find others to vouch for them. There appears to have been a well-organized underground system for passing letters out of Oxford. Most remarkable of all was the claim that men highly placed in the court at Oxford were in the pay of Samuel Luke, and it was even rumoured that Prince Rupert's secretary was a Parliamentary informer paid £200 a month for passing on information. Luke was said to watch the Royalists so closely that 'they eat, sleep, drink not, whisper not, but he can give us an account of their darkest proceedings'. Parliament was itself aware of the danger of Royalist spies and decreed that anyone coming from Oxford or any other part of the king's army without a 'particular warrant' was to be taken 'as spies or intelligencers and proceeded against accordingly'.

Luke's information came from men who were doing their best to be accurate, but one cannot be sure that the same was true of the accounts of events in the news-sheets put out by both sides during the war. These were quite clearly intended as propaganda organs, to boost the confidence of their own side or pour scorn and ridicule on the other. *Mercurius Britannicus* was published in London to present the Parliament view of events and the Royalists, conscious of the damage being done to their cause, answered with *Mercurius Aulicus*, printed in Oxford and claiming to communicate 'the Intelligence and affaires of the Court to the rest of the Kingdome'. It is impossible to know how accurate any of the reports carried in such papers were, but there is nothing subtle about the bias and one can try to allow for it. Antiquarians like Anthony Wood also showed bias, in his case for the Royalist cause. In the case of the treatment of prisoners taken at Cirencester in February 1643 and sent to Oxford by Prince Rupert, it is interesting to compare different accounts of the treatment they received. This is how it was described in a Parliamentary pamphlet entitled *A True Relation of the taking of Cirencester, and the cruell dealing of the merciles Cavaliers towards the Prisoners they there took in their passage as they went to Oxon, and at Oxon.* (The punctuation has been modernized):

> After they had thus taken us, we were led into a field about halfe a mile from the Towne where the chief Commanders were that they might take a view of us, who threatened to do execution upon us all.

And there the common soldiers stript us and wounded many of us, and then drove us back to the Churche in Cirencester, where we remained two whole days and two nights in all. Which time they allowed us no sustenance wherewithall to live, till just as they drove us towards Oxford they gave each of us a small piece of bread and cheese. And then bound us all with match, and so drove us along without stockings on our legs or shoes on our feet or hats on our heads, many of us having no dublets and some gentlemen of good quality without breeches. And so we came to Burford hill, where the Cavaliers gave each of us a little piece of bread, which was all the relief they gave us in our way between Cirencester and Oxon., and for this we waited a long time upon the hill, the wind blowing very cold and we standing barefoot and bareleg'd in the snow. Then we came to Witneigh where we lay in the church and from thence were drove towards Oxon. And about a mile from the city His Majestie with the Prince and the Duke of Yorke came thither to see us drove along more like dogs and horses than men, up to the knees in mire and dirt along the horse way, and aboundance of the scollers, much rejoicing at our misery calling and abusing us by the names of damned rogues and traytors. And when we came to Oxon we were put in the church, and there we received for the most part of us, a piece of bread that night. The next morning they separated the Volunteers from the Trained Bands, and cruelly used us to force us all to take the protestation and take up armes for them against the Parliament, for they allowed us but one small piece of bread and a can of beer a day and would not allow us to have a draught of water to drink, we offering to pay money for it, yet we could not obtaine it. By which cruell usage they forced the most of them to take the protestation.

Anthony Wood's account has a quite different, matter-of-fact tone, mentioning none of the horrors and making the prisoners sound to be all fit and healthy:

Mundaye the 6th of February, about 6 of the clocke at night the prisoners captives, to the number of above eleven hundred, with some 12 or 14 culours taken at Cirencester by Prince Robert

THE
INHUMANITY
OF THE
Kings Prifon-Keeper
At OXFORD.

Or a true Relation of the moft tranfcendent cruelties, cheat-
ings, cozenings, and bafe difhoneft dealings of *William Smith* Proveft
Marfhall General of the Kings Army, againft the *Parliament Prifoners* under his cuftody. As it was delivered at the Barre in the Houfe of Commons, by one, who with many others, were fworne before the
Lords affembled in *Parliament*, and were prifoners in *Oxford*
fix Moneths, being further confirmed by Captain *Win-
gate* in the *Commons* Houfe, he being Member of
the faid Houfe, and fome time prifoner in
Oxford, the fpace of 9. Moneths.

TOGETHER,
With the Copy of a Letter from a Gentleman of quality
confirming the former particulars.

Alfo the Copy of a Petition and Articles exhibited to the
King, His Councell of Warre againft *Smith*.

Likewife a Letter to the Speaker, fubfcribed with 70.
Prifoners hands.

Whereunto is added the unfufferable cruelties, exercifed
upon the *Cirencefter* men, in their paffage to *Oxford*, and
at *Oxford*, in the Caftle and Bride-well, vvhen
they were taken.

Written by Edm. Chillenden. *who was a Prifoner there* 6. *Moneths.*

Printed according to Order.

LONDON, Printed by *G. D.* for *John Bull*, 1 6 4 3.

A pamphlet printed in London in 1643 complaining about the cruel
treatment of Parliamentary prisoners in Oxford Castle.

[Rupert] together with 6 or 7 cart loades of pillage, were brought into Oxford by St Giles his church. His Majestie having byn abroad all that afternoone as farre as Wolvercote, viewed them as they came in, most of them able and lusty fellowes. For that night they were most of them lodged in St Giles his church and Magdalen parish church; from whence they were afterwardes dispersed, some to the Castle, some to other places, etc. And then some of the properest fellowes of them, after they had taken the new protestation appointed lately by his majestie, were new apparelled and tooke into service for his majestie.

As it happens, there is some further evidence which suggests that the Parliamentary account is nearer to the truth. There is a story that a woman in Burford who took pity on these prisoners when they came through the town, and tried to give one of them a drink, was beaten up by the Cavalier guards, and Thomas Wyatt also records their night in Witney and again reports the king's displeasure at the Witney men who showed mercy towards them perhaps by giving them clothing:

Upon Candlemas day . . . prince Robert with a puissant army took Ciceter, pillaged it pittifully. 11 hundred and od prisoners were brought through Witney and then stayed Feb 5th all night and then went to Oxon. . . . Almost all were lodged in Witney church in pittiful manner some maimed carried in cartes . . . February 10 . . . It was reported that Witney men were over kind to the Cicester prisoners, the king heard of it and sent to the town to bring all their clothes to clothe his soldiers that wanted and was offended much with Witney especially with Mr Picsley, but they gave every clothier one cloth and ended.

With so much cruelty happening in the war, it is surprising that there are very few references to rape, which seems to be a much more common fate of women in twentieth-century wars. Whether the lack of reports is because it was indeed a scarce occurrence or because the subject was taboo even for the propaganda press is impossible to say. There are a few references from other places, such as the sacking of Birmingham when Rupert's Cavaliers were accused of being outrageously lascivious and lecherous and 'beastly assaulting many women's chastity' and then boasting about it afterwards, but no similar cases were reported in Oxfordshire, probably because none of the towns in the county was sacked after a siege, which is when such excesses were most likely to happen. No doubt there were other individuals who took advantage of the breakdown of normal rules of behaviour in wartime like the eccentric vicar of Warmington, who left his parish to become a Roundhead cavalry officer but was an embarrassment to his own side. Wyatt recorded that he had been imprisoned in Warwick Castle 'by his brothers in rebellion, for ravishing the Lady Verney's maid'. The women of the Cartwright family of Aynho had a particularly unpleasant time. Sir John was a staunch Parliamentarian and went off to London when the king came into Oxfordshire, leaving his wife behind. She chose the Royalist side and pleaded for her husband at court at the same time begging in vain for him to return. Their house suffered as a consequence of his refusal, by being partially burnt down. Furthermore, his aged mother at Astrop near Kings Sutton was tormented by Cavalier troopers who stuck lighted matches between her fingers and thrust their swords through her dress close to her body before carrying her off to Banbury Castle where she was kept prisoner for about nine months.

Not all women who followed the armies fitted the popular image of camp-followers. Lady Waller, the wife of the Parliamentary general Sir William Waller, accompanied her husband on several of his campaigns and was present with him in Abingdon in 1644. She was much ridiculed by the Cavaliers as 'that preaching lady' because she was an ardent Puritan. The wives of ordinary soldiers also sometimes followed their men to war, cooking and caring for them in the field. A number even disguised themselves as men and fought alongside them. Those left at home coped as best they could and often took the brunt of pillaging and billeting. Little is known about children's experience during this war and one can only imagine the effect of the mixture of exitement, fear and hardship that they must have shared with the rest of the population. The king's elder children, the Prince of Wales and Duke of York, were present at the battle of Edgehill, hiding under a hedge in the care of William Harvey, the royal physician. At one stage the fighting came too close and their retreat to a safer vantage point had to be covered by a Royalist officer. Bulstrode Whitelock's elder sons, James and William, were also saved from potential kidnap by enemy soldiers by a Parliamentary officer in 1645.

One of the traditional roles of women in peacetime was nursing the sick and there was plenty of scope for this during the war. Treatments were derived largely from plants and women were skilled at using these remedies such as they were. Oxford today boasts the oldest botanic garden in England, which was established shortly before the Civil War and was then known as the Physic Garden because of the medicinal use of many of the plants grown and studied there. In spite of this, however, medicine and surgery were primitive and recovery often more a matter of chance. It is thought that some of the wounded at Edgehill survived the night after the battle when they lay on the field untended only because the severe frost congealed the blood from their wounds and prevented them bleeding to death. A military hospital of sorts was set up in Sir Thomas Spencer's mansion at Yarnton in 1643, but most of the evidence for it comes from the number of burials for that year, which is unusually high and includes a number of soldiers. The one happy exception to this is the entry in the marriage register for 14 January 1644: 'William Barlow and Elizabeth Matthews both servants in the Commissarys for the sick here, were married.'

It is impossible to make an accurate estimate of the number of people who died in the Civil War because of the incompleteness of the records. Reports of casualties in any battle or minor skirmish tend to come from the propaganda news-sheets which inevitably exaggerate those of the enemy and play down their own side's losses. Burial registers contain very few entries which can be identified as soldiers, as the large numbers killed in battle were buried in mass graves, unrecorded in the registers. The lack of reference to soldiers in these registers is sometimes very surprising. At Cropredy, scene of the county's largest battle in 1644 when hundreds must have been killed, the burial register of St Mary's Church mentions only six soldiers being buried that year. One is tempted to ask not only where the rest are, but why these six received special treatment. Only one of them is named, Edward Webb, 'manager of the king's horses', the other five are simply recorded anonymously as 'five soldiers'.

Estimates of war-related deaths, however, should include not only soldiers killed in battle but also members of the civilian population, and here the registers are not silent. It is still not possible to distinguish exact numbers of deaths attributable to war and to other causes, but it is clear that there was very high civilian mortality during the war and that much of this was the result of disease, almost certainly spread by the soldiers. Even though the causes of infection were not understood in the seventeenth century it was obvious that disease followed in the wake of armies, and that the overcrowded and filthy conditions that commonly existed in garrison towns must have something to do with it, but the best efforts of the authorities in towns like Oxford were unable to make much improvement. There is ample evidence in contemporary accounts of sickness in the field armies of both sides and this was bound to be spread to the civilian population. Even in an age when cleanliness and personal hygiene were minimal the unwashed, lousy and undernourished condition of so many soldiers was exceptional. They were made susceptible to infection by the extreme physical exertion of long marches in cold and wet conditions, too little sleep and shortages of food and clothing. There were many diseases including bubonic plague which were prevalent in seventeenth-century England and there were recurrent years of high mortality outside the period of the war, but there can be little doubt that the presence of the armies made things much worse for the civilian population of Oxfordshire, and 1643 seems to have been a particularly bad year.

A sample of burial registers which have survived for the period 1636–46 demonstrates this very clearly (see appendix). For these twenty-two parishes taken together, the average number of burials during the preceding seven years was 640, but in 1643 it shot up to 2,029, an increase of 217 per cent, and while there was not an increase in every parish, this pattern is noticeable in very many across the county including a number not included in this particular sample because their registers are missing for some years. Some places stand out: 189 people died in Thame in 1643, whereas the average for the preceding seven years was only 40. A high number of innkeepers were included in this total, presumably a vulnerable group because of the number of soldiers they would come into contact with as lodgers and customers. For Henley, the number of burials leapt to 229 in 1643 from an average of 71. Both Thame and Henley were on the eastern frontier of Oxfordshire and may have been exposed to infection from both sides. It is known that the Parliamentary army under the Earl of Essex was in a particularly bad state when it was in that area in the early part of 1643, having been brought almost to a standstill by sickness after taking Reading. For part of this time Thame was the earl's headquarters. Oxford's plight during the occupation and the heavy death toll there has already been described.

Perhaps Banbury is the town that suffered most, being subjected to two sieges of its castle by Parliamentarians as well as the pillaging by Royalist troops when it was first taken, and here, too, disease played a significant part. The average number of burials for 1636–42 was 86, but in 1643 the total was 253 and it went even higher, to 293, in the following year and was still above 200 in 1645. 1646, the year of its second siege and final surrender may have been as bad but the registers simply stop after February and do not continue until August when the fighting was over, itself an indication of the turmoil in the town. Banbury is also one of those places where the numbers dying of plague are separately recorded in the burial register, so that the evidence of disease among the civilian population is clear. For each month from March through to October there are lists headed 'Theis supposed to die of the plague in this month . . . the day of buriall uncertain.' Many of the deaths in Banbury were of course soldiers from both the Royalist garrison in the castle and the attacking Parliamentarians. Quite often the name of the person in whose house they were billeted is also given: 'a soldier from widdow Kymbals of Calthorp . . . a trooper lodged at Robeart Gaskyn's . . . a trooper from the Whit Lyon', or even sadder: 'a child from the castell . . . a soldier's wife' reminding us that women, sometimes married to soldiers and sometimes not, were also involved and that babies were born amid the horrors of plague and siege.

Plague is a general term used to describe a range of illnesses in the seventeenth century, and while it is probable that bubonic plague was one of the causes of mortality during the war, other diseases were also present. The main one was probably a form of typhus which was then sometimes simply referred to as 'the new disease' for want of a more specific description. In 1643 Thomas Wyatt wrote in his journal that there were 'very many in Oxford and in the shire sick of a new disease. Many died, both soldiers and others in August and September'. A little later he made a more detailed entry which not only gave a more precise name to the disease, *morbus castrensis* the camp fever which clearly linked it with the army, but also included a description of some of the very unpleasant symptoms and stated that there was no effective cure:

> There was a grievous sickness began in the autumn 1643 spreading; many died in Oxon, Witney, Abingdon and other places. Some called it the new disease others morbus castrensis. Their water was as red as blood and continued so 14 and 15 dayes or more. The remedy was abstaining from food, and a coole posset drink with juice of lemons and barly water, but the best phisick was no phisick for as many as were let blood or take vomits died.

It is impossible to make really accurate estimates of the numbers who died as a result of the Civil War, but it has been suggested that perhaps a higher percentage of the population of England and Wales died as a result of this war than were killed in either of the two world wars of the twentieth century.

CHAPTER 6

1643: ROYALIST ASCENDANCY

In the early months of the year there were rather half-hearted peace talks in Oxford when a group of 'Commissioners' appointed by Parliament came to Oxford to offer terms. Whitelock was one of the leading negotiators on this occasion, but nothing was achieved, the king being insulted at the conditions suggested and confident that he could win the war in the field. It was certainly a year in which there was much military activity in and around Oxfordshire, but although most of the successes went to the Royalists, the decisive victory which would end the war was not achieved either here or elsewhere in the country. In Yorkshire the Earl of Newcastle pushed back the Parliament forces under Fairfax, and in the West Country the Royalists under Hopton were reinforced by part of the king's Oxford army under Lord Wilmot, and secured a notable victory over Waller at Roundaway Down. These successes might have led to a concerted effort against London, but instead the armies became bogged down in sieges at Hull and Gloucester.

For the people of Burford any lingering memories of the Christmas festivities were disturbed when at dead of night on 31 December a Roundhead raiding party suddenly burst into their town, and fierce fighting broke out. Sir John Byron had been on his way from Oxford to Stow with a train of artillery and was passing through Burford when he was surprised by the attack. His scouts had given warning that Roundhead cavalry were in the area, but he made the mistake of assuming that they would approach from the Cirencester direction, and placed himself and his main guard at the top of the hill facing that road. Instead the Roundheads skirted around the south of the town and burst in from that side. Fierce fighting took place in the narrow street, Byron endeavouring to prevent them reaching the centre of the town, while he sent the guns away under escort on the road to Stow.

Mercurius Aulicus gives a lively account of this desperate struggle, predictably highlighting the bravery of Sir John:

Sir John considering hereupon that should the enemy possess the Crosse and the houses on either side the streete, it was not possible for him to continue there nor do any service with his horse against them being sheltered and defended, commanded those who were next to follow him, and rushed in upon them laying about him with his sword . . . No sooner was he amongst them but some of those that were furthest gave fire upon him, which doing no hurt they presently broke themselves to flight in a great confusion, some crying that they were for the king and some for Prince Rupert. In this confusion he drave them before him to the further end of the lane where the Inne standeth, into which they ran and into which he, entring pell mell with them, received a blow on the face with a Pole-axe or Holberd, wherewith hee was in danger to have fallen from his horse. But quickly recovering himself againe, hee saw the Inne door full of Musketeers, and himself alone, unarmed and naked of defence in the open street and thereupon turned back to the market crosse.

The rest of his troops followed up the initiative he had gained and chased the Roundheads out of the town, pursuing them for six miles, but failing to catch any of them because 'the night was wondrous darke and the moone not risen'. Byron was left with a large scar on his face which he bore proudly like a battle honour. It shows clearly in the portrait he commissioned from Dobson, painter to the royal court at Oxford. The burial register for the parish church at Burford records the burial next day of six soldiers.

A similar episode occurred on the other side of the county a few weeks later. Parliament forces had moved into Henley and intended to hold it as a forward base from which to threaten Oxford. A counter-attack was attempted by Sir Arthur Aston with troops from the Royalist garrison at Reading, who came at night and tried to surprise the garrison. The attempt failed because the defenders had placed a cannon (presumably loaded and ready to fire) pointing down Duke Street, along which Aston's party approached. This gun was fired at them as they galloped into the town, killing some and scattering the rest. The casualties appear to have amounted to six soldiers 'whereof foure were slaine with the discharging of a canon as they marched up Duck Street to assault the Towne' as the burial register put it. According to one account a local man who had assisted the defenders was wounded and chased by the Royalist as they left the town. Like the fleeing Roundheads at Burford he tried to save himself by crying pro-Royalist slogans, but on both occasions this fooled nobody and he was felled with a blow from a poleaxe.

Rupert had left Oxford in January to attack Cirencester, which he took at the second attempt early in February. He captured about 1,100

Prince Rupert. (Gerard Honthorst, *c.* 1641–2)

prisoners, whose treatment on their cold and hungry march back to Oxford has already been described. This was the first stage in the Gloucestershire campaigns aimed at securing supplies of cloth from Cotswold weavers, iron from the Forest of Dean and ultimately foreign imports through the port of Bristol. Meanwhile, however, he headed north to the Midlands to clear a way for the queen on her return from Holland with troops and armaments bound for Oxford. His sacking of Birmingham and the night of rape, pillage and arson which followed was never forgotten or forgiven by the Parliamentarians.

In the second half of April, Essex laid siege to Reading, and managed to keep his besiegers in place in spite of the cold and wet weather and an attack on them by some of the king's troops from Oxford. Rupert had taken much of the Oxford army with him and so those that were left were reinforced with men from the garrison at Brill, and attacked Essex on the outskirts of Reading. Anthony Wood describes how the local Trained Bands were summoned into Oxford to provide a temporary guard there while the regular garrison was away, and remarks on how unusually quiet it was in the streets of the town with not so much as a drum beat or any trampling of horses hooves. With impressive energy and speed (which was typical of him) Rupert, having moved from Birmingham to capture Litchfield on 21 April, marched back to Oxford where he paused to refresh himself a little and to have dinner, before moving on again to catch up with the king. The relieving force was delayed by Parliamentary cavalry who blocked their way temporarily at Dorchester and there was some fierce skirmishing. Sir Arthur Aston, Governor of Reading, hit on the head by falling roof tiles during Essex's bombardment of the town, was replaced by a less resolute deputy Colonel Fielding, who agreed to a surrender almost as the king arrived. On his return to Oxford he was court-martialled and condemned to death, but reprieved on the scaffold.

The withdrawal of the Reading garrison meant a further increase in the number of troops to be accommodated and fed in Oxford and Abingdon, with all the problems and unpleasantness that this meant both for soldiers and civilians. It was also about this time that the terrible effects of sickness in both armies began to take their toll in many parts of Oxfordshire. Essex's large but ill-supplied force was exhausted and virtually brought to a standstill by camp fever which raged through its ranks. For several weeks it was unable to make any positive move, or to press home the advantage gained by the capture of Reading, while its commander sent urgent messages to Parliament for supplies and money to pay his soldiers. Perhaps unaware of how seriously weakened the Parliamentary army was, the king fully expected an attack on Oxford to be launched, and so made elaborate preparations to counter this, not only by impatiently urging the citizens to complete work on de Gomme's ramparts, but also by setting up an entrenched 'leaguer' or fortified camp on Culham Hill. Lying just to the south of Abingdon and close to the Thames, this was intended to block Essex's advance. The elaborate arrangements proved so much wasted effort as the expected attack did not come, but the pattern of events in this camp, as described by Luke's spies, afford a good idea of some of the problems of keeping a seventeenth-century army in the field, especially when it had to stay in one place for some time.

In early May, as the weather began to feel a bit more like spring, several thousand foot-soldiers, relieved of the fear and tension of more active service, began to settle themselves into their new camp with cheerful enthusiasm and the kind of ingenuity which hardened soldiers develop for making themselves comfortable wherever they are to stay for more than a few nights. Ralph Norton reported to Luke that they were 'making tents of bords and hurdles and have fecht all the beddes out of the country'. The camp was laid out in 'streets' which were even given names like London Street. To ensure supplies of food for such a large number the king issued a proclamation to the people of Thame, Wantage and Faringdon that they must not hold any markets in their own towns, but must bring all their produce to Culham camp. The camp was described as being in a cornfield (which was ruined by the operation), with the river Thames running on the left side and Oxford on the right. On 12 May the soldiers were 'enlarging their workes and making their trenches deeper' and on the 20th they had made '700 caves or hollow places in the wheatfield . . . which some conceive is for their safeguard, others suspect is to destroy our forces as they march that way'.

There was, however, an undercurrent of discontent because the men had not been paid for some time – just how long seems to have been a matter of dispute. The king put on an impressive show which appears to have been an attempt to blind the men with gold braid and which today would no doubt be preceded by much rehearsal of ceremonial drill, inspections and general 'bull'. The Prince of Wales, his younger brother the Duke of York, Prince Rupert and his brother Prince Maurice 'with 3 lords and a countesse' (but which countesse the spy could not say) were sent to Culham to review the troops. The thirteen-year-old Prince Charles made a speech to the soldiers and assured them that his father the king was aware that he owed them just ten days' pay, 'but they report themselves to be seven or eight weeks behind'. The informant concludes 'at two of the clocke that same day all the soldiers received pay, but how much he knows not.'

Yet more troops were withdrawn from the area around Bicester and the eastern side of Oxford and packed into Culham camp. One report states that there were 20,000 soldiers and about 500 tents on the hill, which suggests a degree of exaggeration, (or else the tents were either very large or very crowded). Soon there were other problems. By the time the camp was a month old a serious shortage of food was developing. May and June are difficult months in the countryside, when last winter's stores have been used up and the new summer's crop is not yet ready. Luke's spy reported on 1 June that 'there is great want of provisions upon Culham hill, insoemuch that the soldiers are constrained to drink water, and to rob, pillage and plunder all the country thereabouts'. When the locals complained they were simply told that if Essex came they would lose even more, which gave them little consolation but accurately described the plight of civilians, whichever side they supported. The cavalry were tired of their daily round of patrols as far afield as Blewbury, leaving camp early and returning late, and seemingly never out of the saddle, and soldiers were reported to be trying to desert 'but they were nowe more strictly lookt to by the officers'. Finally, sickness began to spread and, on 10 June, Luke was informed that 'in Abbington and Culham hill there are about 5,000 of the king's forces but so sicke and weak that if they were putt to march it is thought halfe of them were scarce able to march away'. All this is seen through the eyes of the enemy, but the deterioration of conditions and morale in the camp have a definite ring of authenticity.

Although Essex's main army was inactive during May, there had been a very one-sided engagement in the north of the area. This may have been the result of a clever bit of subterfuge by which false instructions, purporting to come from Essex, were fed to Parliamentary troops in Northampton, luring them down to attack Banbury Castle when they thought its commander was away. Equally their attack may have been prompted by the reported burning of many houses in that long-suffering town by its callous Cavalier garrison, angry at the continued hostility of its Puritan inhabitants. The Northamptonshire men were caught in the trap that had been laid for them, and many were slaughtered at Middleton Cheney. Locals who had previously managed to keep their heads down revealed their true allegience by turning out to support the Parliament troops and were laid open to reprisals. One of them wrote: 'We are in more feares than ever wee were.'

At last, at the beginning of June, Essex began to advance against Oxford, but not from the south, as expected. Instead he moved up the eastern side of the county and based himself in Thame. This forced the Royalists to abandon Culham and move troops back into the area around Wheatley, Beckley and the east of Oxford generally. Essex may have pushed forces as close to Oxford as Wheatley, but when on 17 June he attempted to drive the Royalists out of Islip his troops were sharply repulsed. This incident apparently goaded Prince Rupert into one of his most famous escapades, the raid on Chinnor leading to the Battle of Chalgrove Field, certainly one of the best known episodes of the war in Oxfordshire. There may also have been another motive, to intercept a rich supply train carrying more than £20,000 for the Parliamentary army as well as other much-needed equipment, which would undoubtedly have appealed to the Cavaliers. In the event they won a more valuable, but sadder reward. That Rupert was able to carry out the raid with such precision was due to an infamous soldier who changed sides twice during the course of the war, one Colonel John Urry. He deserted from Essex's army (because he felt his services were not sufficiently valued there) and came into Oxford with detailed information about the positions of the various parts of the Parliamentary army, which were widely spread over the country to the east of the city, and in particular a detachment of Sir Samuel Luke's

Bedfordshire regiment (he had an active command as well as being in charge of spies) quartered at Chinnor.

Leaving Oxford in the late afternoon of the same day on which Essex had attacked Islip, Rupert took a force of about 1,700 troops, presumably largely cavalry, and set off at speed to make a circle around the south of the Parliamentary outposts at Wheatley. They crossed the river Thame at Chislehampton and then rode fast through the night ignoring the shots fired at them by the guards in Tetsworth, snatching ten prisoners at Postcombe to prevent them giving the alarm, and were in place in a circle around the sleeping village of Chinnor just before dawn. At 4 a.m. the 'folorn hope' were sent in to flush out his victims, who scrambled and fell out of their beds in cottages, sheds and barns, 'waking only to die' as they were helplessly shot down in the street or trying to flee across the fields. A group of officers who managed to get into a house and shoot at their attackers from the windows were mercilessly driven out by setting the thatch alight, and picked off by the waiting Cavaliers as they ran out of the back door. About fifty were killed and at least a hundred more fortunate ones were taken prisoner.

The alarm had by now been raised, and John Hampden who was sleeping at Watlington hastily gathered what troops he could and, sending urgent messages to Essex at Thame to bring larger reinforcements, set off after the now retreating Rupert in a desperate attempt to cut off his return crossing at Chislehampton Bridge. Rupert, aware of the danger but full of ingenuity, sent troops on ahead to line the hedges and form an ambush into which he intended to draw his pursuers, but Hampden came up on him too fast, perhaps because of the one hundred prisoners, who in spite of being beaten and driven along with all speed must have been an encumbrance to the Royalists. At Chalgrove Rupert changed his plan, turned around and faced the enemy, charging repeatedly against Hampden's smaller force. The Royalist horsemen, although they had by now been riding hard and fighting for many hours, were too strong for the Parliamentarians and the final blow came when Hampden was led off the field slumped over his horse's neck. Rupert was able to continue his withdrawal, making it safely across the bridge before allowing his exhausted but triumphant troops to rest. Later that day they returned to Oxford amid much rejoicing.

The memorial to John Hampden at the site of the Battle
of Chalgrove Field.

The wounded John Hampden, still on horseback, was led towards
Thame, a distance of several miles, in spite of intense pain. It is said
that as he passed through Great Milton he asked for water at one of
the cottages, but was refused as the tenant feared reprisals from his
landlord, Sir Robert Dormer, whose house had already been attacked
by Hampden on an earlier occasion. With greater compassion for his

enemy, the king offered to send his own physician to tend Hampden's wounds, but he died five days later at the Greyhound Inn, where he had lain in great pain for most of that time.

A slightly less romantic version of his wounding at Chalgrove suggests that it was not the result of enemy fire, but the explosion of his own overloaded pistol. John Hampden was undoubtedly one of the heroes of the Parliamentary cause, but was also a good and honest man who was respected even by his opponents.

As for the wagon-loads of money and supplies for Essex's army, these escaped Prince Rupert, being driven up into the Chiltern woods out of sight. According to an intriguing story still remembered in Watlington, however, some of it may not have reached its destination. Hampden apparently spent the night before the Chinnor raid sleeping at an inn in Watlington owned by one Robert Parslowe. He was thought to have had with him a chest full of money to pay his troops, part of the supply sent from London. In the confusion following Rupert's raid and the shock of Hampden's death this chest disappeared. After the war local residents were surprised and suspicious to notice that Parslowe started to buy land and eventually became quite a wealthy yeoman. At his death he founded a charity – was this conscience money?

Following this set-back Essex withdrew his army into Buckinghamshire, moving his own base from Thame to Aylesbury, and the immediate pressure was taken off Oxford. Royalist forces ranged about the area, re-establishing their control, and the newly knighted Sir John Urry attacked and pillaged High Wycombe. More importantly, the way was kept open for the queen with her reinforcements and supplies to make her way safely to Oxford from the north. Rupert went from Oxford through Woodstock and Chipping Norton to meet her coming from Stratford and escort her the rest of the way. A joyful reunion between the king and queen together with the Princes Charles and James, was arranged at Edgehill, they spent a night at Wroxton and then headed for Oxford where the queen was greeted on 14 July with a lavish welcome from the loyal university and perhaps slightly less enthusiastically by the representatives of the city.

Replenished with the supplies brought by the queen, Rupert now set off to Gloucestershire again and laid siege to Bristol which he captured before the end of the month. It was a very important gain, securing a major port for the Royalists and thus making it much easier for them to receive foreign support. Its value was fully appreciated by Parliament, and they condemned its garrison commander Nathaniel Fiennes for surrendering the city too easily. He was reprieved from the death sentence, but lived to see the irony of Prince Rupert also being disgraced for exactly the same reason when Bristol was recaptured from the Royalists in 1645. After Bristol the Royal army turned its attention to Gloucester and on 10 August settled down for another siege. Parliament sent orders to the Earl of Essex to take his army to Gloucester and relieve the city by driving off the besiegers. He was given reinforcements and set off slowly with a very large army towards the end of the month.

Rather surprisingly his route took him across north Oxfordshire, south of Banbury, through what was supposed to be Royalist territory. It became clear, however, that with the main Royalist army at Gloucester, the troops left behind with Rupert and Lord Wilmot were not sufficient to stop his relentless progress. Once again the local inhabitants found themselves trampled over and robbed of whatever they had left, demonstrating once more that it made little difference which side they were on. Although strengthened by the addition of London Trained Band troops, the Parliamentary army was soon in trouble, not so much from the harassing of the enemy, but through shortages of food and lodging for so large an army in an area already sripped bare by the Royalist garrisons.

Marching with one of the Trained Bands was Sergeant Henry Foster who left a very clear picture of the privation they suffered as they crossed the north of the county from near Brackley through Chipping Norton to Stow-on-the-Wold, two places notorious for cold, in an unusually wet and cold early September. (The account consistently calls Stow 'Stow the Old' which must have been a soldiers' nickname for it.) On 31 August they were at Stratton Audley where there was 'little provision either for officers or soldiers'. Essex kept up his men's morale by reviewing the whole army of fifteen thousand troops and 'there was great shouting and triumph as he passed by to take a view of our regiments'. From here on, however, they were constantly harassed by Royalist troops, but were not drawn into a pitched battle. There was some fierce fighting around Deddington and Clifton where Wilmot tried to stop them but was driven back to Banbury. Essex was quartered at Aynho while Sergeant Foster's regiment was at the tiny village of Souldern 'where our six regiments that came from London were quartered' (about five thousand troops). Not surprisingly they were 'very much scanted of victualls in this place'. On 2 September they were at Hook Norton where again the whole brigade quartered. There was more skirmishing with Wilmot, and a few soldiers were killed, mainly Cavaliers according to Foster. The effect of this harassment was not only to slow down Essex's progress, but to increase the tension and discomfort for his men, already desperately short of food. The constant threat of attack, even if it did not come, kept them on the alert and, together with the bad weather and lack of accommodation, meant that they could not sleep properly either. It was in these circumstances that one of the worst attrocities reported in Oxfordshire took place in Chipping Norton. Foster's regiment had marched through Chipping Norton where they met up with the main body of the army on a 'great common' about half a mile from the town, and were then sent on ahead to quarters near Oddington. The best lodgings had all been taken and so they had to go on even further. They now found themselves out in an exposed position ahead of the main army:

> having not so much as one troope of horse quartered neer us . . . but we were no sooner in our quarters, and set downe our armes, intending a little to refresh ourselves; but presently there was an alarme beat up, and we being the frontier regiment neerest the enemy, were presently all drawn up into a body, and stood upon our guard all that night. We were in great distraction having not any horse to send out as scouts, to give us any intelligence . . . Our regiment stood in the open field all night, having neither bread nor water to refresh ourselves, having also marched all the day before without any sustenance, neither durst we kindle any fire though it was a very cold night.

The main body, with Essex himself, was camped in and around Chipping Norton where those not under cover in the town also endured a miserable night of cold and hunger standing tired and nervous in the open, fearing an attack at any moment out of the darkness. According to a report in the Royalist news-sheet *Mercurius Rusticus*, as these tired and hungry soldiers were leaving the town the next morning, a woman among the crowd watching in the market-place rashly shouted out a pro-Royalist slogan, 'God bless the Cavaliers!' Incensed by this final insult on top of all their discomforts of the night, they broke from their ranks and dragged her out of the crowd. Then,

> they tied her to the taile of one of their Carts, and stripping her to the middle, for two miles march whipped her in so cruel a manner with their Cart whips that her body in many places was cut so deep as if she had been lanced with knives, the torment being so great (as much as her straight bonds would give leave) she cast herself on the ground, so to shelter her self from their stripes, but in a most barbarous manner they dragged her along, in so much that her leggs and feet were torne by the Stony rough wayes that her flesh was worne off in many places to the very bones.

Somewhere down the other side of Cross Hands hill they cut her loose and left her for dead at the side of the road, where perhaps her family – her husband or her children who may have seen what happened – dared to come and find her and carry her back to Chipping Norton, where she died.

There is no corroboration that has survived from other sources for this incident, but the circumstances of the march and the condition of the troops is documented, and our knowledge of the brutalizing effect of such conditions and of war generally, make it likely to be true. It was almost certainly not the only incident of its kind.

As soon as the army reached Stow, the Trained Band regiments at least, who were ahead of the rest, got some refreshment, but were suddenly aware of a strong Royalist force of cavalry under Prince Rupert which threatened to surround them. According to Foster, Rupert missed a great chance to cut them off from the rest of the army and destroy them. In characteristic Puritan style he put this merciful deliverance down to the Lord. There was skirmishing and quite a lot of posturing and threatening rather than actual fighting throughout the rest of the day. The Parliamentary artillery and the superior size of their army forced Rupert to give way and some of his troops were chased from the field and pursued until it was dark. Sergeant Foster and his comrades, with a little food and an easy victory under their belts, were better able to endure the hardship of another night in the open 'on the plowd-land, without straw, having neither bread nor water'.

Essex's army now moved away from Oxfordshire making its painful way towards Gloucester, but there were yet more hardships to suffer on a stormy night when some waggons were toppled over in the darkness on the hill above Cheltenham 'it being a most terrible tempestuous night of winde and rain as ever men lay out in', and alarms given twice during the night 'in the midst of all the storme and raine, which together with the darknesse of the night made it so much the more dreadfull, which also caused great distraction among our souldiers, every one standing upon his guard, and fearing his fellow souldier to be his enemy'. Indeed one young soldier was mistakenly shot in the confusion. The shortage of food and drink continued: 'We had by this time marched six daies with very little provision; for no place where we came was able to releeve our army, we leaving the road all the way, and marching through poore little villages; our souldiers in their marching this day would run halfe a mile or a mile before, where they heard any water was.' Sergeant Foster's graphic account is written from the viewpoint of the soldiers, but what of the 'poor little villages' who were not only unable to relieve the army, but would presumably have had nothing left to eat themselves after such a ravenous horde had passed through – and this just before the onset of winter? These later passages refer to events outside Oxfordshire, but they very clearly illustrate the hardships facing soldiers and civilians everywhere in this war.

Essex's eventual approach forced the king in great dejection to raise the siege and withdraw from Gloucester. As he fell back towards his Oxfordshire base he attempted to prevent the Parliamentary army returning to London by attacking it near Newbury. Another rather inconclusive fight ensued, the first Battle of Newbury, in which neither army was destroyed, but Essex was able to continue to London. After

The memorial to Lord Falkland near the site of the first
Battle of Newbury.

the battle the king strengthened the garrison in Donnington Castle making it an important stronghold guarding this southern route.

The great loss to the king in this battle was the death of Lucius Cary, Viscount Falkland. He had been Charles' Secretary of State for just more than a year and his advice was appreciated by the more moderate members of the Council as a counter to the fiery Prince Rupert. It was his advice to the king, however, that may have led to his death. That the manner of his death was suicidal, riding straight into enemy fire where he was bound to be killed, was generally agreed, but there were two opinions about the cause. Clarendon records that he had become morose and melancholic some time before the battle, and it was thought that he blamed himself for advising the king to besiege Gloucester, which now seemed very bad advice. John Aubrey in his *Brief Lives* has a typically scandalous alternative, which was that he was overcome with grief at the death of a mistress, a fine lady of the court, with whom it was claimed he was passionately in love. Whatever the truth of the situation, Falkland's death was sadly lamented and his body was brought back to Great Tew, where the register records his burial in solemn and formal style on 23 September 1643. No memorial was erected at the time and the site of his grave was unmarked, lest Parliament sympathizers should desecrate it. There is now a memorial on the south wall of the chancel of the church that was erected in the nineteenth century.

Before the campaigning season ended, the Royalists reoccupied Reading with a strong garrison under Sir Jacob Astley, greatly strengthening their position in the Thames Valley. However, as the troops went into their winter quarters in Oxford and Abingdon there were the usual complaints from the inhabitants. Many had died this year, and although winter brought some lessening in the number of deaths each month, they did not cease. Abingdon, now quartering additional foot-soldiers as well as Rupert's Cavalry, complained that they were cutting down standing trees for firewood. In the closing days of December John Harris, a carpenter in Adderbury, burning with Puritan zeal, made his personal protest against the Cavaliers and their High Church ways, perhaps especially directed at Adderbury's own Royalist vicar, Dr William Oldys. He went into Adderbury church and ripped up the prayer book, and then did the same to the Bible.

CHAPTER 7

1644: ESCAPE TO CROPREDY

There were no major military engagements in Oxfordshire during the early part of 1644. Two contrasting lines of activity were being pursued during these months. In Oxford a pro-Royalist parliament had been summoned, consisting of lords and MPs who were loyal to the king, and they were concerned to persuade him to find a negotiated solution to his differences with the 'rebel' Parliament in London. Since the latter saw itself as the only true and legal parliament and refused to recognize the 'Oxford' assembly there was little hope of progress towards peace talks. The king was himself disappointed at the line taken by this supposedly loyal body in Oxford, from whom he had no doubt hoped for more positive support, and he eventually prorogued it in April.

Meanwhile, military matters had not been at a standstill. There was much backward and forward movement of troops especially in the north-eastern quarter of the county. Rupert, with Colonel Urry, who seems still to have been in high favour, attempted an attack on Aylesbury but got nowhere, the defenders and the weather combining to defeat them. Even an unsuccessful action such as this may have seemed a relief from the discomforts and tensions of winter quarters in Oxford, where a captain had been shot for stabbing another senior officer and there had been an attack on the governor, Sir Arthur Aston, in the darkened streets one night. A spy reported that the wound was likely to prove fatal 'which the generallity of the city pray for'. He was wrong about the wound but probably right about the prayers. It was known that Parliament was reorganizing its forces and was planning a concerted effort against Oxford, which was expected to come from the eastern side as before. The attack on Aylesbury had hoped to forestall and impede this advance. Now there were strong forces placed in and around Bicester, and Luke's spies sent back endless reports of troop movements which mention Wendlebury, Baynard's Green, Brill, Weston-on-the-Green, Boarstall, Stanton St John and Watlington, showing that there was activity all down the eastern side of the county facing Parliamentary Buckinghamshire. The queen's troop of horse was stationed at Wheatley, keeping a close guard on the bridge and making it difficult even for Luke's men to get through to Oxford without questioning, searching and sometimes temporary imprisonment. Henley was still in Parliamentary hands and so the Royalists put much effort into strengthening the defences of Greenland House. In return, the Roundhead Major-General Skippon took charge of the unruly garrison at Bulstrode Whitelock's Phyllis Court in Henley, constructing massive earth defences and extending the moat. Parliamentary Oxfordshire, Buckinghamshire and Berkshire were formed into an association so that their combined resources could be coordinated and directed to the forthcoming assault on Oxford. Throughout the rest of Oxfordshire, which remained in Royalist control, the locals concentrated on getting through the winter with whatever depleted stores the armies had left them, while still being ordered to pay their weekly contributions and being spasmodically plundered by neighbouring garrisons.

At the beginning of April the decks were cleared and both sides prepared for more serious action. The queen had been in Oxford since the previous July and had enjoyed being together with Charles all through the winter, which would have done much to make life in the overcrowded city more bearable for both of them. Now, however, she was pregnant and Oxford was under threat, and so it was decided that she should leave. They went as far as Abingdon together, and then parted for the last time, she going towards the West Country and eventually to France after the birth of their daughter Henrietta in Exeter, and he back to Oxford to decide how best to meet the expected attack. There were divided opinions on this, Rupert recommending strong outlying garrisons to keep the enemy away from Oxford, but Charles eventually deciding to withdraw troops from some of these more distant towns to strengthen Oxford itself and the forces immediately around it. Rupert himself was off to campaign in Lancashire, and his absence gave Parliament's forces the opportunity they needed.

The Earl of Essex and Sir William Waller were ordered to take both their armies and advance on Oxford, but they were no doubt pleasantly surprised to find the Royalists abandoning first Reading and then Abingdon, as they fell back on Oxford. Withdrawing the garrison from Reading was intentional, part of the king's plan to concentrate his strength closer to Oxford, but Abingdon was abandoned as the result of a disastrous mistake or misunderstanding of his orders by Lord Wilmot. The king's instructions were to defend the town, which was clearly vital to the defence of Oxford, but at the approach of Essex Wilmot drew his men out and allowed them to retreat to Oxford themselves, perhaps feeling that Abingdon was indefensible in spite of having about six thousand foot-soldiers in the town and a large contingent of cavalry which could have been brought up from Faringdon. By the time Charles heard what was happening it was too late to do anything about it. Essex seems to have been so surprised at finding the town undefended that he paused outside it all night, while the frightened inhabitants waited anxiously to see how they would be treated by this new occupying army.

Abingdon was taken on 26 May and Essex moved with unaccustomed speed to encircle Oxford. He moved to the east side of the city, crossing the Thames at Sandford on the 28th and then advancing though the little villages of Littlemoor, Church Cowley, Temple Cowley and Headington. Between the last two he drew up most of his army in battle array on the open space of Bullingdon Green, facing Oxford in a threatening gesture in full sight of its defenders, the king watching the whole procedure from the top of Magdalen Tower. This was both a show of strength and a precaution to deter any attempt by the garrison to attack his army from the side while it was on the move. In particular, it protected his artillery and baggage waggons which were moved ahead behind the screen thus provided by the rest of the army. After this they picked up the line of what was in the seventeenth century the main London–Worcester road between Stanton St John and Islip, where the first opposition was encountered. Essex's objective was a crossing of the Cherwell so that he could cut off the north-eastern routes to and from Oxford, and the first of these was at Gosford Bridge. Fighting took place on 29 May with a Royalist regiment which had been positioned in Islip; they

Sir William Waller, the Parliamentary commander
defeated at Cropredy.

managed to defend this bridge and prevent a crossing being made for several days.

Meanwhile Waller had taken his army around to the west of Oxford to block up that side, intending eventually to meet up with Essex, having completely surrounded the king and trapped him in his capital. While Sir Jacob Astley defended the Cherwell crossings, the king sought to prevent Waller's part of the plan by attacking his base at Abingdon, which he much regretted losing to the enemy, and by a similar defence of the river crossing at Newbridge near Standlake where Waller's army attempted to get across the Thames. Thomas Wyatt had witnessed 'many thousands of horsemen' coming through Ducklington and quartering around Black Bourton and Brize Norton as soon as Essex came to Abingdon and now a detachment of cavalry and dragoons previously based at Charlbury was quickly moved down to reinforce these troops in holding the bridge at Newbridge. They were successful in withstanding Waller's first attack on the 27th. The Royalist newsheet *Mercurius Aulicus* claimed that the demolition of Abingdon's fine medieval cross which happened at this time was an act of spite occasioned by the failure at Newbridge, but is more likely to have been simply another expression of Puritan hatred for anything they considered superstitious or Papist. Less damage was achieved by the king's attack on Abingdon late on 29 May which was beaten back.

Pressure was increased on the crossings both to the east and west of Oxford, Essex spreading his forces over several potential crossing points near Bletchingdon, Enslow Bridge and Tackley Ford, as well as Gosford Bridge, all of which Sir Jacob Astley was desperately trying to hold, while

A tranquil scene at Newbridge. It is very different from the day when the Revd Thomas Wyatt wrote anxiously of 'much ado about Newbridge' as fighting raged around this vital crossing point on the Thames, before Waller forced his way across in June 1644.

Waller renewed his attacks on Newbridge. Tension must have been mounting in Oxford, and one can certainly sense the anxiety which Thomas Wyatt felt in his rectory in Ducklington, so close to the action at Newbridge. He was also aware that Waller's Parliamentarians would treat him far less respectfully than the worst Royalist troops he had so far experienced. He writes anxiously of 'much ado about Newbridge' which he hears has been partly pulled down, and he openly states 'my fear was of the parliament soldiers coming towards us'. On 2 June the breakthrough happened and Waller's men came flooding into the area, pillaging as they went, as the Royalists fell back to Oxford. 'There came some to Ducklington June 2 and took from me a very fine gelding and a year-old good colt, a good young mair and my old great mair that I used to ride on and Sir William Waller and Mr Fisher and the constable promised to restore them but deceived me.'

Later the same day the king ordered Astley to abandon the Cherwell bridges and withdraw his men to Oxford. Essex brought his army across and came to Woodstock only hours after Charles himself had left it, having somehow found time and sufficient detachment from the urgency of military affairs to hunt there that day and reputedly kill two bucks. By 3 June the circle around Oxford was almost complete, Essex was at Woodstock and Waller reached Eynsham, with the only remaining gap the few miles between those places. Clearly there would have been very great anxiety felt by many people in Oxford, both in the king's council and among the citizens, and probably among some of the soldiers too. Some understandably advised surrender while generous terms were still a possibility, and an interesting sideline on this is that Parliament itself was distrustful of its own commander, fearing that Essex would agree some compromise instead of pressing home his advantage. The relationship of the nobility to the king must have made even men like the Earl of Essex suspect, and rumours were obviously flying around, one of which Thomas Wyatt picked up in Ducklington when he wrote at the height of this crisis that 'it was reported from Oxford very seriously that Essex had kissed the king's hand and would come to him with 2000 soldiers'. As it was, Charles refused even to seek terms and instead planned and executed an amazing escape from the trap rapidly closing around him.

On Sunday 3 June he assembled the core of his army in front of the city's defences in the region of Port Meadow, having hurried back from Woodstock the night before and slept in his coach close to the troops. The artillery and some of the army were sent off in the direction of Abingdon, again threatening Waller's base, which caused him to send troops back in that direction and diverted his attention from the king himself who, with the remaining cavalry, set off at about 9 p.m. in the summer dusk and marched through the night. Using lanes and fieldways, meeting up with some of his foot-soldiers waiting at Yarnton, and then proceeding via a route known to the locals going to market as Froggledown Lane, he made his way with all these troops towards Hanborough Bridge which was reached safely by the morning. They were now within a very short distance of Essex's men at Woodstock and Waller's at Eynsham, and that such a manoeuvre could be carried out with several thousand horse and foot-soldiers without alerting the enemy is hard to believe. Hanborough Bridge was crucial as it was the only available crossing of the Evenlode and allowed the Royalists then to speed away towards Witney. Two other tricks had been played on the Parliamentary forces to draw their attention away from the escape. Another feint had been made in the direction of Abingdon on the morning of 4 June, and the danger of losing such an important prize so soon after it had been captured must indeed have drawn Waller's attention in that direction. To fool Essex, the colours of the Royalist regiments were left stuck in the ground amid the other soldiers still in front of Oxford's defences to make it look as if the whole army was still there. This subterfuge and the Royal army's surprising speed and even more surprising silence, secured their escape. After resting briefly near Witney it headed to Burford, Bourton-on-the-Water and away to the safety of Worcestershire. Waller heard too late of their move, and pursued them in vain to Witney, catching only a few stragglers. That he was at Ducklington on the evening of 4 June is confirmed by Wyatt, who says he lodged with Sir Arthur Haslerig 'at Mr Bailies', but that 'Sir William Waller went away about 10 a clock in the night'. Clearly there was some hasty dashing about after the king and no doubt some red-faced confusion. Wyatt is typically more concerned about the cost of retrieving horses requisitioned by the soldiers, but he notes that 'The king (as is reported) went towards Worcester and Waller's army followed him.'

Essex's behaviour now, and the ease with which the king had given him the slip, must raise the question as to whether he had indeed connived at the escape and was secretly relieved that he did not have to inflict the final defeat on the king, in just the same way that the other noble Parliamentary commander, the Earl of Manchester, was to let him off the hook at Newbury later the same year. Essex moved from Woodstock to Chipping Norton and held a council of war with Waller, which consisted of Essex ordering him to follow the king single-handed into Worcestershire, while he headed off down to Devon and Cornwall to join in the campaigns there, thus abandoning the Parliamentary advantage of superior numbers in the Oxfordshire region.

In the next few weeks the Royal army marched and countermarched, gathering reinforcements, and soon made its way back to Oxfordshire. The king's object had been to draw Waller away from attacking a depleted garrison at Oxford and to avoid a confrontation if possible until Rupert could return from the north to reinforce him. So far he had been successful. By 18 June he was back in Witney and Wyatt was again entertaining Royalists at the rectory, though in very large numbers and perhaps he was a little disappointed that the top people lodged in Witney, merely ordering him to send his choicest food for their enjoyment, while he had to put up with the riff-raff:

> June 18 1644 an infinite number of foote and some horse came through Ducklington towards Witney. I had at my house about an hundred that had victuals . . . There was billeted Sir Jacob Astley and his lady etc. but they came not, stayed at Witney the King being there, and the quarter master, one Busby, sent for provisions from us: veal mutton poultry and pigeons and provender for their horses. We had about a dozen that supped and lodged that night, these soldiers all about us stole calves and sheep and poultry and what they could lay hands on. The foote were pitifully ragged and lowsy.

The king left Witney on 21 June and went first to Woodstock and then on into Buckinghamshire, with Waller trailing him. On 29 June,

Cropredy's pre-Reformation eagle lectern, with its
slotted beak said to be for papal contributions. Tradition
records that parishioners saved it from the approaching
Puritan army by dropping it into the river Cherwell
before the battle of Cropredy Bridge.

heading north up the east bank of the Cherwell he saw Waller's army
keeping pace up the Oxfordshire side. As the Royalists became
stretched-out, a gap of at least a mile developed between the forward
and rear sections of their army. Waller saw his chance to cut off their
rear from the rest of the army. Meanwhile the churchgoers of
Cropredy, on the approach of a Puritan army, took their precious pre-

Reformation eagle lectern out of the church and dropped it into the river for safety.

Waller sent part of his army to cross Cropredy Bridge while he took the rest a little south to make another crossing at Slat Mill where there was a ford, intending to separate the Royalist rear and attack it in front and behind. The response they met at both crossings was much stronger than expected, however, and they were driven back, still holding the bridge at Cropredy around which the fighting now concentrated as the Royalists tried unsuccessfully to batter their way across. Fighting lapsed as darkness came, and although both armies retained their positions throughout the following day as well, the Royalists eventually withdrew because strong Parliamentary reinforcements were coming from Buckingham under Major-General Browne. They left the field unchallenged as victors in that their losses had been few, whereas Waller lost perhaps 700, many of whom were deserters, and had lost his artillery. Indeed his army was now so demoralized that it virtually disintegrated. On the Sunday morning he had suffered another indignity in a comical episode at Great Bourton where a council of war was held in the manor-house. The rotten floor collapsed under the weight of the meeting and Waller and his senior officers crashed into the cellar below. It had been a bad two days.

The king headed back across north Oxfordshire from Aynho to Chipping Norton and thence to Moreton-in-Marsh. His next move was to follow Essex to the west and to defeat him too at Lostwithiel in Cornwall, but in spite of these triumphs news of the very serious defeat of Prince Rupert at Marston Moor in July was to prove much more significant in the long run.

Such was the confusion caused by poor communications even at this stage of the war, that a completely inaccurate account of the engagement at Marston Moor reached Oxford, reporting that the battle had been won by the Royalists. Bonfires were lit in the streets and there was much celebration until nearly a week later the terrible truth of Rupert's defeat became known.

July also saw the fall of Greenland House, the Royalist stronghold that had been disrupting communications by river from Henley to Reading and London. The garrison held out successfuly for some time, having been strengthened on 8 July by Sir Thomas Lunsford who brought in extra supplies to help them withstand a siege, but Major-General Browne, the recently appointed commander of the Parliamentary troops in the area, brought up his heavy artillery and began to bombard Greenland from the opposite bank of the river. They managed to score a direct hit on the magazine causing a huge explosion, which together with other serious damage made it impossible for the defenders to hold out any longer. Browne allowed them to march out and retire to Oxford without weapons. The capture of Greenland made the Parliamentary position in Henley much more secure.

More important still, though less sucessful, was the siege of Banbury Castle in the north of the county. The king having moved away from Oxfordshire after Cropredy Bridge, Parliament attempted to recapture this vital stronghold. Troops began to assemble in the area towards the end of July, but before the siege proper began a curiously medieval event took place. According to *Mercurius Aulicus*, forty Parliamentary cavalry under Captain Clark gathered in front of the town and were faced by an equal number of Royalists from the castle garrison under Lieutenant Middleton. After posturing and threatening each other for some time, the two rival commanders goaded each other into agreeing to fight a personal duel. Their supporting troops drew back to watch as the two men prepared to settle the matter with pistols, but the atmosphere of farce was increased when both weapons failed to fire. However, they drew their swords and Clark was wounded (according to *Mercurius* while running away) and then rescued by some of his men. Middleton himself, proudly victorious on this occasion, was killed three weeks later in a sortie from the castle.

All of this happened during the 'softening-up' period of the siege, when the main objective was to cut off supplies to the castle before the bombardment and eventual assault commenced. Parliament knew that by confining the garrison within the castle they would also cause considerable inconvenience to the Royalist headquarters at Oxford, who relied on the Banbury garrison to collect the weekly taxes and other supplies from this northern part of the county. It was reported in London that 'This Castle is of more concernment to Oxford than any other, for besides the provision of victuals by droves of sheep and beasts weekly, it is upon good ground aver'd that for a long time this garrison hath paid £8000 per weeke to Oxford, divers towns being taxed to more than the yearly revenue of them; so that the taking of this Den of Theeves would much conduce to the straightening of Oxford, and give liberty of trade to London from many parts.'

In the last week of August Parliament brought up its heavy guns, and managed to move troops into the town at night to take up positions nearer to the castle. They took over the parish church and positioned guns there as well as using the vantage point of the tower to snipe at the defenders, and even to kill some of their cattle. There was fighting in the streets and in and out of the houses. About thirty houses were burnt down by the garrison to prevent their attackers using them as cover. They also kept up a constant fire of musket and cannon to prevent Parliament setting up their siege guns, which they were consequently forced to do at night. The effect of this situation on the townspeople can be imagined. The siege became something of a personal contest between the two commanders, John Feinnes for Parliament and young William Compton for the Royalists, and both siege and defence were conducted with vigour and determination. It says something for the strength of Banbury Castle's walls that in spite of constant battering from close quarters they, and the defenders, still kept the besiegers at bay. All this depleted Fiennes' stocks of ammunition and he had to request further supplies from Parliament as well as asking for more men to strengthen his assault. Compton carried out repeated sorties, which may have inflicted some damage, but did more to keep up his own troops' morale.

Fiennes then called in a party of miners who were set to work to undermine the castle walls, a technique frequently used in sieges. In this case, however, it availed nothing because their tunnels were quickly flooded with water. This was followed by an attempt to drain the castle moat, but in spite of their best efforts and reports in London that the castle was about to fall, the Parliamentarians were making little progress. They now had to contend with a further difficulty, disease, which began seriously to affect both soldiers and townspeople as the dismal evidence of the burial register records. A concentrated bombardment of the walls opened up a large breach in the outer wall and on 23 September Fiennes attempted an assault at this point. Two accounts exist, one very detailed one in *Mercurius Aulicus* from the point

The plight of ordinary people caught up in the siege of Banbury Castle: a
page from the burial register in 1644 lists those dying of plague each
month. Other deaths in the town include James Hawkins 'slaine with a
bullett from the Castle'.

of view of the victorious Royalists, and a much briefer Parliamentarian one from the *Perfect Diurnal*. They tell the story of the assault on the castle, but also demonstrate how the propaganda news-sheets elaborated, and perhaps exaggerated, good news while they were nearly silent about bad news. *Mercurius Aulicus* claimed that twelve Troopers from each Roundhead company were offered a bonus of £300 to undertake the dangerous task of leading the attack. It continues:

> The number of assaylants was about 1000, they came on with burdens of furrs [furze] on their backes, which they cast into the mote the better to passe the mud, and so assaulted it in several places at once. The greatest number were on that side where the breach was, on all other parts they brought ladders, but the courageous defenders never suffered them to rear so much as one ladder, but cut them off with great and small shot, which was sent among them like haile. Those that defended the breach performed their partes with as much valour as can be imagined, hewing them down as fast as they attempted entrance. All this while the Rebells played upon the upper part of the Castle with great shot, shooting also many grenadoes. But at last the Rebells, seeing themselves unable to do any thing, but undoe themselves utterly, gave off, being so sore beaten, so many killed and wounded, that they were ready to quit the siedge. Towards evening that day they sent a trumpet to desire the bodies of their dead, which was granted upon condition, that those which had fallen within pistol shot of the Castle, should be stript by those of the garrison, and delivered naked in the Market place, which was done accordingly.

This last condition is a reminder that the clothing of casualities was a valuable prize of war.

The Parliamentary account is much briefer:

> The siege of Banbury is gallantly maintained, our men keeping the enemy in continuall action shew themselves experienced souldiers both by their assaults and batteries having made so wide a breach of the Castle, that at least 12 men may march in a breast, which some

too venturously endeavouring to enter received some repulse, but made an honourable retreat to their workes againe.

In spite of this repulse, Fiennes continued the siege for a further month and the plight of the garrison in the castle became increasingly serious. Their only hope of relief lay with the king's army which was far away besieging Plymouth. It was not only Banbury that was threatened, as Parliament had also taken the opportunity presented by the absence of the royal army to attack Basing House and Donnington Castle, two other important strongholds which threatened their supply lines. In mid-October Charles moved back towards Oxfordshire, being near Newbury by the 22nd. The Banbury garrison was by now nearly starved, having resorted to eating their horses, and was on the point of surrender. This would have been an even greater disaster for the king than the loss of Abingdon in May and to prevent it he was forced to send three regiments under the Earl of Northampton to the relief of Banbury, but in the process weakening his own army, now threatened by the approach of a much larger force under the Earl of Manchester and Cromwell. The final betrayal of his weak position to the enemy came from none other than the infamous Colonel Urry who chose this moment to change sides once more. The Royalists lost the second Battle of Newbury on 27 October because of this weakening of their army, but might have suffered a much greater defeat had it not been for the characteristic reluctance of Parliament's noble commander, the Earl of Manchester, to press home their advantage and inflict the final blow on the king. Such reluctance stemmed partly from a traditional sense of loyalty to the monarch, however misguided, and partly from growing fears about what the alternative might be if men like Oliver Cromwell became too powerful and carried through political, religious and perhaps social reforms.

Meanwhile Northampton, reinforced with a regiment which joined him from Oxford, succeeded in driving off Fiennes and his besieging forces from Banbury, attacking them at Easington and driving them beyond Hanwell. The garrison was relieved, exhausted and hungry, but triumphant. They were down to the last two horses for food and it was said that their nineteen-year-old commander, the earl's younger brother, William Compton, had not been to bed throughout the long siege. Whatever the state of the garrison, that of the townspeople was worse after a fourteen-week siege in which they had been caught between the two forces. Many of their homes had been destroyed and nearly three hundred burials were recorded in the registers for the year, the highest total for several decades, almost certainly mainly the result of plague and other wartime diseases. This figure probably does not include every death, but even so it represents nearly 19 per cent of the town's population. The parish church had been severely damaged and its tower nearly destroyed as the building had been used as a gun emplacement by the besiegers.

The suffering of the people of Banbury and surrounding villages did not end when the siege collapsed, as the Royalist garrison immediately set about repairing the castle's defences and restocking it with supplies, at the expense of civilians in the area who were forced to provide labour, equipment and provisions that they could ill afford. 'The enemie hath brought in very large victuall and supplie into Banbury Castle, which they have robd and pillaged the countrey people thereabouts of and undone them, Plundering many to the very walles, especially some honest people in Banbury.'

Like the Royalists in Banbury Castle, so the Parliamentarians at Compton Wynyates practised plunder and extortion on the poor inhabitants of these north Oxfordshire parishes. *Mercurius Aulicus* published the following order from the notorious Purefoy of Compton Wynyates in March 1645, but it was nothing new: 'To the Constable of Shetford and the Inhabitance there. Upon paine of plundering, imprisonment and other extremities I charge and command you bring into my garrison at Compton all my contribution due from the 22 of November to the 4 of March, at one pound five shillings a weeke, by the 7 of this instant: expect not one houre longer time. At your perils.'

In the following year the *Moderate Intelligencer* carried this wry description of the plight of people in the area:

We heare not of any designe prosecuted against Banbury: that place scowers us still a dowzen miles round. The countrey men have a pretty observation, which is this: They say, they pay contribution on both sides: when Banbury men come to gather their mony, they observe a time when their enemies from Northampton are at home, then come they in, and with a loud cry, say, where are these Roundheads? wee'll kill them all for raysing money of you, you shall pay to none but us: when Banbury men are gone, then comes the other party, where are the Cavaliers? wee'll kill them all, you shall pay to none but us, we will protect you; but hardly in a yeare doth the one interrupt the other's collection.

For several months during the summer and autumn of 1644 the king's main army had been absent from Oxfordshire and the Oxford garrison had had its own preoccupations culminating in the terrible fire of 8 October. This must have changed the situation in parts of the county and allowed the Parliament forces to move about more freely in normally Royalist areas. One hundred and fifty of John Fiennes' men besieging Banbury even made a raid to the very outskirts of Oxford, bursting in to the church at Wolvercote in the middle of Sunday morning service on 1 September. They were apparently intent on capturing 'a gentleman of quality' who was in the congregation, but were foiled, although they did succeed in carrying off the 'Duke of York's dwarf'. The Royalist account of the episode ridicules the Roundheads as usual and treats the whole affair as a joke, but it must have been a severe shock to the tiny congregation gathered in their village church. On leaving Wolvercote the raiders galloped to Water Eaton and kidnapped Lady Lovelace from the manor house. Bundling her into her own coach they drove her off as far as Middleton Stoney where, no doubt tiring of the game, they abandoned her, taking the coach with them back to Banbury. Such events achieved little in military terms, but they served to terrorize local people and greatly increase their feeling of insecurity.

By mid-November, in spite of his defeat at Newbury, the king was back in the Oxford area. Banbury and Donnington had been relieved for the time being and it was the turn of Parliamentary Abingdon to feel insecure. Its new commander, Major-General Browne, had been complaining to Parliament for some time, and continued to do so, about the weakness of the defences and the need for more troops to reinforce the garrison if he was to hold this vital town against repeated Royalist attempts to regain it. A fierce attack by 1,600 troops from Oxford had only just been repulsed in early August just before he took over and he poured out complaints and demands for supplies of men and money for several weeks in an attempt to get his superiors to see the seriousness of the situation. Not only did he have too few men, those he had were unpaid, ill fed and mutinous. At least one was shot following a court martial; others deserted. At one stage he reported as many as five hundred sick and some had even died of exposure in the streets of the town. The state of the garrison inevitably had its effect on the population of both the town itself and surrounding villages who were subjected to taxation, pillage and theft of their own food and belongings, and even the inmates of the almshouses had a reduction in their allowance. Browne apparently felt some sympathy for the plight of local people but could do little about it in the short term. Understandably, he several times offered his resignation as governor, but his commendable determination and energy gradually brought some improvement. For some weeks he played a dangerous game of subterfuge, pretending to conduct secret negotiations for surrender with the Royalist Lord Digby. This succeeded in gaining time for strengthening Abingdon's defences. Reinforcements and supplies of money and clothing began to arrive in December and work on the defences was completed at about the same time. They were nearly put to the test before the end of the month when some Royalists took possession of a large house belonging to the Speaker of the Commons, William Lenthall, at Besselsleigh close to the town. They were driven off and the house was wrecked in an effort to make it less useful to the enemy, but the threat of a major attack on Abingdon remained, and the attempt was made less than two weeks later.

CHAPTER 8

1645–6: BLOCKING UP BANBURY AND OXFORD

Major-General Browne had good reason still to be anxious about the situation at Abingdon and its ability to withstand a concerted attack from Oxford. Only a few miles from the Royalist headquarters and controlling a crossing of the Thames, it was a huge threat to the king if it stayed in enemy hands or a safeguard for his survival if he could recapture it. Its defences consisted of a line of 'works', probably banks and ditches, erected to the north of the town under the direction of a military engineer called Kulemburg (also a Dutchman like de Gomme employed by the king in Oxford), and the strongly defended main bridge across the Thames to the south. The garrison was now stronger and in a better state than it had been a few months earlier, but was still small by comparison with the forces at the disposal of the Royalists from Oxford and the various other garrisons in the region such as Faringdon and Wallingford.

In the early morning of 11 January 1645 Prince Rupert organized an attack on Abingdon from two directions at once. He led the main force across Culham Bridge and advanced along the causeway to attack Abingdon Bridge itself, while a detachment of cavalry approached from Faringdon. These did not get very far, meeting stronger opposition than they expected near Drayton and being chased back to their own base. The attack on the Culham side came closer to success. Even if he was unable to enter Abingdon, Rupert would have considered it a sufficient prize to hold on to Culham as a base for further attacks. Unfortunately the winter flooding of the ground on either side of the causeway between Culham and Abingdon Bridges restricted his horsemen who became easy targets for the resourceful Browne's infantry wading in the floodwater to fire at them from both sides. Browne continued the fight as the Royalists fell back to Culham and after three hours of close fighting extending into the fields and hedgerows around the village, succeeded in turning Rupert's retreat into a flight back to the safety of Oxford. Culham Bridge was recaptured, and a serious blow dealt to the Royalists through the killing of General Gage during the final retreat. He was a soldier of considerable experience and skill and had recently been appointed Governor of Oxford.

Browne's victory was followed by the other event for which he is usually remembered, the hanging of five Irish prisoners in the market-place at Abingdon. The fear and hatred of Irish Catholics by the English led to an order by Parliament that they were not to be allowed 'quarter' if captured fighting in the king's armies. Indeed the recruitment of Irish soldiers by the king (even though some of them were Protestants) had aroused objections from otherwise loyal Royalists in England. Browne, in the excited and vengeful atmosphere immediately after the fighting, ordered the killing of these unfortunate prisoners, which Royalist reporters characterized as 'Abingdon law – where trial follows execution'. Another twist in the story of religious hatred was the discovery by archaeologists in 1989 of a Civil War graveyard in Abingdon, in which a number of Cavalier dead had been buried lying in a north–south direction, instead of the customary east–west arrangement. This may have been intended as a final insult to supposed High Church Anglicans.

Although 1644 had brought important victories at Marston Moor and Newbury, Parliamentary morale was surprisingly low during the following winter because of increasingly fierce disagreements among their military and political leaders and between the adherants of the different shades of religious practice which were emerging. These divisions reduced the effectiveness of their organization and even of their armies in the field. In spite of the victories, many of their troops were ill paid, resentful and inclined to desert in large numbers. Waller and Cromwell saw the need for a more professional army with well-trained soldiers led by commanders chosen for their ability and commitment to the cause of defeating the king, rather than their social rank or religious conformity. Such a change was coming, but it would take time, and meanwhile there was pessimism about the outcome of war and a strong argument for peace negotiations with the king, which eventually led to the Treaty of Uxbridge and brought about a short truce lasting for most of February.

The treaty did not stop all military activity. Around the main garrisons in Oxfordshire the opportunity was taken to strengthen their positions and, truce or no truce, the customary foraging and collection of 'contributions' to supply the soldiers' needs had to continue. From Abingdon, Browne was ranging far afield disrupting Oxford's communications and intercepting its supplies – six butts of Canary wine on one occasion and some carriages and sixty horses taken near Shotover on another. Blagge was doing much the same around Wallingford, and it was in January 1645 that he carried out the raid on Long Crendon from which he was fleeing when Anthony Wood witnessed the exciting pursuit of his men past the vicarage in Thame. He also recorded, two months later, a raid on some Parliament troops in Thame by men of the Boarstall garrison. These used to visit Thame regularly, 'and would watch and be upon the guard in the vicaridge house . . . and continue there a whole night together. Some of these troopers would discourse with the schoolboys that lived in the house . . . that which A.W. observed was that the vicar and his wife were always more kind to the parliament soldiers or rebels than to the cavaliers.'

There was a lot of activity around Banbury. Not only were the defences of the castle itself being repaired, but the Royalists were very busy in the area strengthening other houses, intent on making it difficult for Parliament to mount another siege. There was a regiment of horse and fifty musketeers based on Lord Wilmot's house at Adderbury, and the Roundhead Sir John Cartwright's house at Aynho was seized and garrisoned, a drawbridge being constructed between it and the village, although this apparently did not stop its Royalist garrison spending their days drinking in the town, where Luke's spy thought they could easily be surprised.

Rousham, built by Sir Robert Dormer in the 1630s, had already been plundered together with the more humble dwellings of the villagers in 1644, and now it was occupied by a small troop of Cavaliers, who cut gun-slits in the great door to facilitate its defence. (Although the house has been enlarged and much altered since then, the door is still there.)

In the last days of January, while the Treaty of Uxbridge was being signed, Sir William Compton's men from Banbury launched a fierce attack on the rival garrison at Compton Wynyates. Their rivalry was particularly bitter, not merely because they were close to each other and vied for supplies from the same sad area of south Warwickshire and north Oxfordshire, but because the beautiful Warwickshire house was Compton's own family seat, seized from his brother the Earl of Northampton by Colonel Purefoy the year before. After some hours of fierce fighting among the stables and outworks of the house, the attackers were driven off with some loss of life.

On a national level the initiative in these first months of 1645 definitely lay with the Royalists because Parliament was preoccupied with the reorganization of its army. Old commanders were removed and new ones appointed and a 'New Model Army' was being formed out of the remnants of the old ones, first by asking for volunteers, but soon through conscription because too few men came forward. The new army was to be thoroughly trained, disciplined and prepared to fight in any part of the country, not just in its own local area. All this took time, however, and Parliament was anxious that the king should not be able to take advantage of its temporary weakness before the New Model Army was ready to take the field. Cromwell was sent into Oxfordshire to keep the Royalists busy, and in particular to try to prevent the king joining up with Rupert and thus concentrating their forces for an attack. Cromwell's advance into Oxfordshire was also the first stage of Parliament's campaign to destroy the king's base at Oxford by 'blocking it up' – cutting it off from external supplies and eventually capturing the city, 'Having found by experience for three years past that the advantage of that place situate in the heart of the kingdom hath enabled the enemy to . . . infest all other parts.'

Towards the end of April he came storming into Oxfordshire from the eastern side and defeated three regiments commanded by the Earl of Northampton based at Islip to guard the bridge. Reinforcements were sent from Wallingford but arrived too late. That evening Cromwell moved on quickly to Bletchingdon, one of a line of fortified manor houses where the king had placed garrisons to delay the advance of an enemy approaching Oxford from that side. He moved so quickly that the garrison was taken by surprise, although they must have known of the action at Islip earlier in the day as about fifty of the fleeing horsemen had taken refuge with the garrison. In command of Bletchingdon House and its garrison was Francis Windebank, son of one of Charles' close advisers before the war. Less than two years before, on 2 August 1643, the register of Wolvercote parish church records his marriage to Jane Hopton. She and some other ladies were with him at Bletchingdon on the night when Cromwell's horsemen suddenly appeared outside and made a peremptory demand for the surrender of the house. An instant reply was required and either delay or refusal would bring an immediate attack with no quarter for those inside. Windebank, fearful for his young wife and the others in the house, and doubtful of receiving any relief from Oxford in time to save them, negotiated terms for surrender. Bletchingdon was handed over to Cromwell in the early hours of the morning and Windebank took his wife and the garrison back to Oxford unmolested but disgraced in the eyes of many of the army. As might be expected, he was not well received by the king, who ordered him to be tried by the council of war. He was found guilty of surrendering an important stronghold without attempting to defend it and was condemned to death. On 3 May, in spite of many pleas to the king for mercy, Francis Windebank was shot against the walls of Oxford Castle. His wife's feelings can only be imagined.

Cromwell, meanwhile, had continued his rapid campaign, spending only one night at Bletchingdon and the next day marching across the county to attack Royalist troops at Witney and Bampton. On 26 April he approached Faringdon, but here he was stopped. Faringdon House, on the outskirts of the town, was well positioned and strongly defended. It had been an important base for Royalist troops and something of a threat to Abingdon. When Cromwell summoned it to surrender, its commander, Lieutenant Colonel Burgess replied: 'We will have you know you are not now at Bletchingdon . . . we fear not your storming nor will have any more parleys.' Cromwell battered it for several days, causing considerable damage to houses in the town which were occupied by his troops during the attack and therefore in turn were battered or burnt by the Cavaliers themselves, but he could not achieve his objective. Faringdon's church, with its magnificent spire, was within the defences and inevitably received a battering. The

The stump of Faringdon's tower still lacks its spire, demolished during
Cromwell's attack on the Royalist stronghold in Faringdon House.

south aisle and transept were severely damaged by a direct hit from a
Parliamentary cannon, and at one point the spire was in danger of
collapsing into the moat. The defenders feared that this would create
a kind of bridge of rubble across the moat and so mined the tower
themselves, making it fall in a safer direction. When the Pest House,
about 300 yards from the walls, was occupied by fifty musketeers,
Captain Gwynne led a sortie from the house to dislodge them and
succeeded in killing or capturing nearly all of them. In the end
Cromwell had to withdraw and what was left of Faringdon remained
in Royalist hands until June the next year, when it was included in the
same agreement as Oxford.

The manoeuvres of the last few weeks had been successful in
confining the king to Oxford as he did not feel safe in venturing out
while Cromwell, now supported by Browne and the Abingdon
garrison, was so active in the area. Early in May, however, he emerged
and took part of his Oxford army to meet up with Rupert at Stow-on-
the-Wold. Cromwell went after them and harassed the rearguard as it
was leaving Burford. There were two burials of soldiers in Burford on
8 May which may have resulted from this encounter. One of Prince
Rupert's officers died of wounds and John Bullock, farrier in Lord

The Siege of Oxford, painted by Jan de Wyck in 1689. It has been suggested
that it is meant to represent the siege of 1645 when William Legge was
governor of the city, although being painted so long after the event it is
innacurate in some details.

George Goring's regiment which had been sent to cover the king's
march, was 'shott by his fellow soldier' – perhaps a case of 'friendly
fire'.

Charles' intention was to campaign in the Midlands and north
during 1645, leaving the garrison in Oxford to look after his base there
until he returned. Almost as soon as he had left, however, Parliament
sent orders to Fairfax to join Cromwell and Browne in Oxfordshire and
set about reducing Oxford itself. On 22 May the three commanders
began to establish siege lines around the north of the city. Fairfax based
himself at Marston, Cromwell at Wolvercote and Browne at Wytham.
The Oxford garrison had already withdrawn within the defences, and in
doing so took the usual action to make sure that the attackers did not
have the benefit of buildings close to the works which would give them
cover. Houses at Hinksey and Wolvercote were destroyed and Godstow
House itself set on fire, but the latter attempt was foiled by
Parliamentary troops who were able to quench the flames and preserve

part of the building. Water as well as fire was used in the city's defence, the low-lying meadows on the west and south of Oxford being flooded to prevent attack from those quarters.

There appears to have been some fighting all around the city, described in *Mercurius Aulicus* in its usual sardonic style: 'The Rebells offered to have gained Master Smith's House standing without the workes on the South side of Oxford, came often creeping up, and for their paines were buried in Hinksey churchyard. Divers rebells were also killed by the Horse and Musketiers on the North and East part of Oxford.' The governor himself led a successful sortie against the troops dug in on Headington Hill in the early hours, killing about ninety and taking fifty prisoners. The besiegers had a small revenge the same evening when they sneaked up to the walls and drove off some cattle grazing outside the East Gate 'through the negligence of the guard'. *Mercurius* reached a peak of sarcasm when reporting a request by Fairfax to the Governor of Oxford for an exchange of prisoners 'although,' said Sir Thomas, 'tis not usual to exchange prisoners in a siege. The Governor sent him thanks for his seasonable intelligence, for till then he never had any notice of a siege, there being not one Alarme ever given to the garrison during all the 15 dayes Sir Thomas lay near Oxford.'

In spite of the upbeat tone of their propaganda, the garrison and courtiers in Oxford were far from confident of their ability to survive, being very short of food and other stores. This first siege commenced on 22 May and by 3 June the Council found it necessary to start releasing their stocks of grain to relieve the poorer inhabitants. The king's Secretary of State sent him an urgent request for help. It was the last thing he wanted to hear while busy campaigning elsewhere and he did not respond immediately. Ironically, it was not the wish of Fairfax to be sitting down in front of Oxford, he would have preferred to pursue Charles and try to destroy his army in the field. Meanwhile, he obeyed his orders, and began to construct a breastwork on Headington Hill and made a bridge across the Cherwell near Marston to allow his troops to move freely around the north side of the city, from Headington to Wytham.

The Parliament army did not, however, confine itself to encircling Oxford. In order to ensure the isolation of that city from its sources of supply elsewhere in the county, attacks were launched against some of these outlying strongholds. On 1 June Gaunt House near Standlake, close to the crossing of the Thames at Newbridge to the west of Oxford, was captured by Colonel Rainsborough. Boarstall House, so long a thorn in the side of Parliamentary forces on the Buckinghamshire–Oxfordshire border, managed to survive a fierce twelve-day siege and remained in the hands of its Royalist garrison. *Mercurius Aulicus*, doing its best to keep up morale among the Royalists, made the most of this success, recounting the great number of 'granadoes' and cannon shot vainly fired at the house: 'Wednesday they playd hotter than before, shooting that day 22 Granadoes and cannon shott so thicke as not easily numbred, besides volleies of musketeirs.' This kind of bombardment maintained over several days was intended to soften up the garrison and create breaches in the walls before the final assault, but before this was launched the convention was to give the defenders a last chance to surrender by sending a formal 'summons' delivered by a trumpeter. Fairfax sent a very courteous but firm summons to Sir William Campion commanding the garrison at Boarstall:

> Sir,
> I send you this Summonse, before I proceed to further extremities, to deliver up to me the House of Borstall you now hold, with all the Ordnance, Armes, and Ammunition therein, for the use and service of the Kingdome, which if you shall agree unto you may expect civilities, and fair respects, Otherwise you may draw upon your self those inconveniences which I desire may be prevented. I expect your answer by this Trumpet within one houre. I rest
> Your servant
> Tho: Fairfax.

According to *Mercurius* Campion's reply was scornful and defiant, concluding 'I am therefore ready to undergoe all inconveniences whatever, rather than submit to any, much less to these so dishonourable and unworthy Propositions. This is the resolution of Sir, your servant, W. Campian.'

The inevitable outcome was an assault by Fairfax's troops: 'They fell on about 12 on Wednesday night, storming the House in every place for full three houres, but were most gallantly repulsed by the brave Loyall Garrison, who were infinitely heightened to see their valliant Governour upon his crutches visit all the Batteries . . . The Rebells brought with them six score scaling ladders but the caseshot and musket poured so thicke upon them that they left all them behind.' After a further bombardment the attackers sought a 'parley' and truce to carry off their dead. 'The parley continued 2 houres, after which they gave good store of Cannon shot and 4 Granadoes for a farewell, and then drew off marching away in great disorder.'

The real reason for the withdrawal was that Fairfax had received the orders he had been hoping for, to leave Oxfordshire and go after the king, who had been campaigning in the Midlands and had captured Leicester a few days before. Fairfax quickly abandoned not just Boarstall but the siege of Oxford itself, and headed north with Cromwell.

The king's intention had been to head further north himself to defeat the Scots while Fairfax and Cromwell were still tied up elsewhere, but he had been forced to delay in the Midlands by the pressure put on Oxford, and the urgent requests for assistance he had received from the court there. His response to these was in turn to put pressure on Parliament by threatening its garrisons and communications, hence the attack on Leicester. He then sent a supply column to replenish Oxford consisting of large flocks of cattle and sheep rounded up in Leicestershire and Northamptonshire, but to get them there safely he had also to send an escort of 1,200 cavalry. Unable to proceed with his own campaigning without this force, he waited a week for their return, giving Fairfax's army time to catch up with him. The result was the Battle of Naseby, fought on 14 June, in which Charles was severely defeated by the New Model Army, and his own army virtually destroyed. His artillery was captured, as was his baggage train containing among other things, copies of his personal letters to the queen. These were gleefully published by the Parliamentary press, not only to embarrass the king but to show that he had been negotiating to bring an Irish army over to fight his English opponents.

It is generally accepted that Naseby was the decisive battle of the Civil War, after which the king had little chance of recovery, having lost his main army. Charles himself seemed unwilling to accept this, being full of optimism based on a religious conviction every bit as strong as Cromwell's, that God would not allow him to be defeated by the rebels. This was the extent of his belief in the 'Divine Right' of kings. After Naseby he headed for the Welsh borders where he felt he had the best chance of raising a new army, visiting Oxford for only one day towards the end of August.

Oxford's garrison was still capable of some positive action, and on 7 September Thame was the scene of another skirmish witnessed by Anthony Wood. A number of Parliamentary horsemen had been stationed there and were surprised with a sudden attack by the Oxford garrison led by their adventurous governor Colonel William Legge, his brother Robert and David Walter the High Sheriff of Oxfordshire:

> Before they came neare to Thame, they divided into two bodies, the van headed by Colonel Walter and the reer by Colonel Robert Legge. They found the towne very strongly barricaded at every avenue: notwithstanding which Major Medcalf . . . gallantly led up the folorne hope, charged the rebells' guards and maintained his ground so handsomly that major Aglionby coming up to his assistance the rebells were beat off the guards, so as major Medcalf with 7 troopers leapt from their horses, and removing the carts, opened the avenue. This done the two gallant majors charged the rebells up through the street, doing execution all the way to the market-place, where col. Greaves himself stood with about 200 (Parliament) horse drawn up; but col. Walter being ready with the other troops . . . gave the rebels such a charg as made them fly out of the towne.

The cavaliers then began searching out Roundhead soldiers who had tried to hide in houses and stables, and some from the vicarage who took refuge in the church. Many were caught and taken prisoner but the main objective was plunder of their equipment and belongings. Anthony Wood and his schoolboy companions enjoyed their own share of booty on this occasion, eating the venison pasties left in the oven of the vicarage kitchen by its Roundhead occupants when they were surprised by the sudden attack.

Legge then led his troops back towards Oxford, but a couple of miles out of the town a body of two hundred Roundhead cavalry who had regrouped came up and attacked them from behind. 'Col. Legge charged them so gallantly that the rebels ran back much faster than they came on. Yet farr had they not gone, before these vexed rebels came on againe; and then also col. Legge beate them so farr back that they never attempted to come on againe.' In this last clash a young Royalist captain, Henry Gardiner, was shot and killed. The tragedy was the greater because his elder brother Thomas had also been killed a month before. They were buried side by side in Christ Church Cathedral. Wood assessed the losses on both sides with his usual disdain for 'the rebels', but also a typical distinction between the ranks on his own side: 'Besides this gallant gentleman, no other officer was killed, only three common soldiers . . . the rebels dropt plentifully in the street and in the fields.'

In this same month of September an incident tinged with both tragedy and comedy occurred in Adderbury. In spite of the threatening influence of Lord Wilmot of Adderbury, one of the king's generals, there had always been a strong Puritan element in the village, and it was perhaps this which forced the vicar, Dr William Oldys, to leave his parish for the greater safety of Banbury Castle. It was from there that he set out one morning to escort his wife and son on their way to Oxford. 'Escort' is perhaps not quite accurate for, fearing an ambush, he sent them on ahead with instructions to wave and warn him if they saw anyone lying in wait for him – presumably they were satisfied that his family would not be harmed. His fear was well founded, for having just passed through Adderbury on the way south to Oxford, some Roundhead soldiers were seen waiting to seize him. Warned by his wife, Dr Oldys turned his horse round and gave it its head to gallop back towards Banbury. Unfortunately his faithful horse, knowing so well the way back to its stable in Adderbury, raced there instead and the desperate doctor could not pursuade it to go further. The soldiers easily caught up with him and shot him dead. On 15 September he was buried in his own church and the register records briefly and accurately that he was 'murdered by the rebels'.

Away from Oxfordshire Parliamentary forces were intent on capturing remaining Royalist towns and fortresses. Their most significant success was the recapture of the port of Bristol, held by the

The memorial in Adderbury church to its Royalist
vicar, Dr William Oldys: 'a strenuous upholder of the
threatened cause of religion and majesty, struck down
by rebel soldiers near this town, 1645, aged 55'.

Royalists since 1643 and one of their main links with the Continent from
which supplies of men and arms might be hoped for. Its garrison was
commanded at this time by Prince Rupert himself, but even his
experience and daring could not hold it. He negotiated a surrender
which allowed him to bring himself and his troops out safely and back to
Oxford, but these generous terms, on top of the disastrous surrender of

such an important city, led the king to suspect treachery and Rupert was stripped of his command and ordered to leave the country, although he was eventually exonerated and reconciled with Charles. Such dissension in the Royalist camp must have been an even greater encouragement to the increasingly confident Parliamentary armies. In October Cromwell captured Winchester and finally subdued Basing House which had held out for the king for so long. The king returned to Oxford in the first week of November and stayed there throughout the winter.

The winter of 1645–6 must have been a bleak one for the king in Oxford. Even his optimism must have faltered as his chances of a military recovery faded. He still pinned his hopes on reinforcements being found in Wales to build a new army and Sir Jacob Astley was dispatched to gather such a force and bring it to Oxford. At the same time Charles was negotiating with the French ambassador, Montreuil, who was in Oxford until 3 April. The cavalry regiments from Oxford went out into Wiltshire and Dorset raiding the countryside but doing nothing to alter the inevitable course of the war. At the end of February a party of Cavaliers temporarily occupied Cumnor church, using it as a lookout post, and when they left they are reputed to have stolen the weathercock from the top of the tower.

It was now only a matter of time before the Parliament armies returned to besiege Oxford. There is not much evidence to show how the people of Oxfordshire greeted this prospect. The courtiers in Oxford had apparently been relieved that the king had stayed away from the city in the months after Naseby, for they feared his presence there might have brought the Roundhead armies to besiege them. They must have known now that such a fate could not be long avoided. The City Council was still bickering with the king over money and especially his request that a tax should be levied to pay Thomas Dennis (one of their own members who was loyal to the king) some money said to be owing to him. They resolved 'to make such answer to his Majesty as shall be advised'. In March they renewed the agreement allowing the king the hay crop from Port Meadow for the cavalry, but this year they added a significant proviso that should the war end and the garrison be disbanded before the hay harvest the agreement would be cancelled and the crop revert to the citizens. For most of the citizens, especially those with property to lose, there would be an incentive to surrender and save what they could, while for the soldiers of the garrison, especially the senior officers, their training and instinctive loyalty to the king's cause would incline them to resistance and a last-ditch stand. Throughout the towns and villages of Oxfordshire Puritan sympathizers may have looked on the advance of the Parliamentary forces as a welcome liberation from Royalist occupation, but many innocent civilians would be caught up in the struggle, suffering the usual hardships of billeting, taxation, requisition and plunder, although the reputation of the New Model Army in this respect was much better than that of the Cavaliers. For known Royalists the prospect was obviously worse. It was during the early months of 1646 that the Revd Thomas Wyatt had his worst experience of billeting by Parliamentary troops at Ducklington described as 'the most unreasonable that ever we had . . . spent and spoiled as much as was possible in so short a space'.

Part of the plan for the final siege of Oxford was to seize all the outlying garrisons and strongholds that had done so much to sustain it throughout the war. Donnington Castle was besieged through the winter and in January Colonel Whalley moved into Banbury to begin a second siege of the castle. He continually complained that he needed more men and guns and in February the *Moderate Intelligencer* reported that 'The design against Banbury sluggs for want of supplies and necessaries.' The castle was still defended by Sir William Compton who again carried the attack to his besiegers by launching sorties against them whenever the opportunity presented itself. They were also harassed with raids by horsemen from the Oxford and Woodstock garrisons, and Whalley had several times to divert his energies from the siege to deal with them and in the end found it necessary to dig a trench encircling the whole town behind his own positions to protect his rear. The castle at Banbury was clearly a very strong fortress with at least two moats surrounding high, thick walls which had been strengthened with banks of earth. The Puritan Joshua Sprigge gave it a grudging respect when he described it as being 'old in time, yet recovered and revived by art and industry unto an incredible strength, much beyond many places of greater name and reputation'. Such strong defensive works together with the energy of its garrison foiled all attempts to take it. When Whalley's men dug trenches towards the walls to undermine them, the defenders replied by

The Abbey Gateway, Abingdon. In March 1646 earth
and rubble piled in the road near here was all that
prevented the Royalists penetrating to the centre of the
town in their last desperate attempt to recapture it.

countermining those trenches, and when they approached the walls
above ground they were met with a hail of rocks and stones as well as
bullets. Not until the political and military situation of the Royalist cause
elsewhere had deteriorated beyond recall did Compton finally agree to
surrender terms.

It was still the king's aim to strengthen the position of Oxford by
recapturing Abingdon, and a further concerted attack on it was made

at the beginning of March. Just as the sentries on duty all night were withdrawn, a strong body of cavalry surprised the guards on the defences around the north of the town and burst through driving the defenders back through the streets. They forced their way as far as the Abbey Gateway, where only the lack of shovels to clear the earth and rubble that had been piled there to prevent access prevented them going further. Very fierce fighting took place in which the desperate efforts of Browne's defenders, supported by many of the inhabitants, eventually regained the upper hand and drove the Royalists back out of the town. The attack was renewed a few days later but was no more successful, the attackers no longer having the advantage of surprise, and Abingdon remained in Parliamentary hands. Barton House was burnt down and one side of Radley Church demolished during this fighting on the outskirts of the town.

The king now planned to take his remaining forces out of Oxford northwards towards Chipping Norton to meet up with the new regiments recruited in Wales and the borders by Sir Jacob Astley. His last hope, such as it was, rested on these inexperienced soldiers who were now approaching Oxfordshire. The hope was dashed when news reached Oxford that Astley's reinforcements had been completely defeated and dispersed or taken prisoner at Stow-on-the-Wold on 21 March, the last battle of the Civil War. Sir Jacob Astley had fought loyally for the king since Edgehill, when he had been credited with the famous prayer 'Lord, Thou knowest how busy I must be this day. If I forget Thee, do not Thou forget me', and he closed the last battle with that other memorable saying addressed to his Parliamentary victors: 'You have done your work, boys; now you may go play, unless you fall out among yourselves.'

News of Astley's defeat came hard on the heels of similar news from the West Country where the last Royalist forces under Hopton had been defeated and the remaining garrisons were being taken by Fairfax, who was soon able to turn his own attention towards Oxfordshire again. Donnington Castle at last surrendered at the end of March, although Banbury and Woodstock were still holding out. Woodstock Manor had been surrounded by Colonel Rainsborough since mid-March, but was strongly defended by Captain Fawcett. An assault was made on 15 April at six in the evening, but was beaten

Stow-on-the-Wold, whose streets witnessed much coming and going of
armies, and near which the last battle of the war was fought when
reinforcements coming to the relief of Oxford were defeated in 1646.

back with the loss of many lives and more scaling-ladders. The
bombardment went on for several more days, no doubt clearly audible
to the Royalists confined in Oxford, which must have been a very
worrying sound to the citizens at least. Finally, on 26 April terms were
agreed and Woodstock surrendered, the garrison being permitted to
go to Oxford, but without weapons.

The day after this, 27 April, the king had his long hair cut short,
dressed himself 'in a Montero with a hat upon it', and left Oxford for
the last time, disguised as a servant. He was playing his last desperate
card banking on being able to play off one faction on the
Parliamentary side against another. Riding in this disguise with three
other men who addressed him as Harry, the 'royal' party made their
way secretly via Nettlebed and the woods near Henley, but then
turned north and some days later the king surrendered himself to the
Scottish army at Newark.

The king's flight and surrender did nothing to alter the fate of the
remaining Oxfordshire garrisons, being a political rather than a

military manoeuvre. Parliament was anxious that it should not deter its armies from finishing the job of destroying Royalist strongholds. General Fairfax, having completed his campaign in the west, arrived in Oxfordshire and took up quarters around Garsington on 2 May ready for a full-scale siege of Oxford. Other infantry regiments were quartered in the villages around the city on 3 May and a rendezvous was held on Bullingdon Green. The next day Fairfax called a council of war and plans for the siege were agreed.

Parliament's Committee of Both Kingdoms had voted large supplies of money and equipment to ensure success this time. The list of siege equipment included 1,200 wooden spades and shovels, 300 steel spades and 500 pickaxes, for digging trenches and perhaps mines under the walls and for throwing up their own defensive earthworks. There were 200 sets of horse harness and twenty carriages for provisions, a small number to supplement those waggons already in use and no doubt others were to be requisitioned from the surrounding villages. Finally, in order to batter the city into submission, there was a plentiful supply of ammunition: 500 barrels of gunpowder, 1,000 hand grenades, 600 grenado shells, 30 tons of bullets, 40 tons of match and 200 scaling-ladders for the final assault.

It seems that Fairfax made more use of the picks and shovels than the gunpowder and grenadoes. He decided at the outset that Oxford was not going to be taken by a quick assault, being strongly fortified, having an experienced garrison of between 3,000 and 5,000 troops and being well stocked with provisions and supplies of powder and ammunition. It may be that Fairfax was also reluctant to cause too much damage to the medieval buildings of the ancient university (of which he was himself a former member), and perhaps he simply wished to avoid unnecesary bloodshed now that the outcome of the war was inevitable. It has been suggested that he may have exaggerated the strength of Oxford and its ability to withstand a siege, in order to justify to his political masters the need to negotiate and to agree fairly generous terms. His experience as a commander and his own nature probably made him prefer to obtain his objective with as little expense of money and lives on his own side as well as the enemy's, rather than seeking to punish his opponents in revenge for the last four years of war, the policy which appealed to some others in the army and in Parliament.

He began by constructing camps protected by defensive works for his besieging forces at Headington, Cowley and to the north of the city. These were necessary in any well-conducted siege because the garrison would not remain passively inside their walls, but would both bombard the besiegers and seek to attack them on the ground in sorties whenever possible. On 11 May a formal summons was sent in to the governor, demanding surrender of the city. It included the statement from Fairfax that he 'very much desired the preservation of that place (so famous for learning) from ruin, which inevitably is likely to fall upon it except you concur'. Sir Thomas Glemham, the governor, did not agree to surrender, but he seems to have found himself in a very difficult position between different factions within Oxford. Since the king had left, the governor had somehow to reconcile, or overrule, the conflicting wishes and interests of the Lords of the Privy Council, individuals like Prince Rupert, the soldiers and officers of the garrison and the citizens of Oxford. The Privy Council and the citizens were generally in favour of surrender, while the governor and garrison wanted to fight on. The Privy Council established its authority on behalf of the king, and Glemham issued a statement disclaiming any responsibility for the decision to discuss terms with the enemy which he said had been forced on him. The first cannon shots fell in Christ Church Meadow, fired from Headington Hill, and arrangements were agreed for a meeting of 'Commissioners' from both sides to discuss terms in Mr Croke's house at Marston on 18 May.

Banbury Castle had already surrendered ten days before. The terms agreed between Sir William Compton and Colonel Whalley were generous to the garrison in recognition of their spirited defence and the undoubted strength of the castle itself, which would have allowed them to go on defending it for much longer if they had chosen. The surrender was apparently accompanied with a surprising amount of cheerful goodwill on both sides, the Royalists being permitted to march out and given passes to go to any other place in England apart from London or any place under siege (i.e., Oxford) or 'beyond the seas'. The common soldiers were even offered 'free quarter, marching ten miles a day' on their way home or wherever else they chose to go. The trumpeter who announced to Parliament the news that the

Banbury garrison had agreed to surrender was given a reward of £20 as an expression of their pleasure!

Oxfordshire's other remaining Royalist garrisons had all been summoned to surrender and were being 'blocked up' by Parliamentary troops. These included Faringdon, Radcot, Shirburn, Boarstall and Wallingford where Blagge was resisting all attempts to take the town, and threatened to set the whole place on fire if the Roundheads approached too close. Both Blagge and Glemham in Oxford would have liked to have been allowed to communicate with the king and seek his permission to surrender, but this was refused on the instructions of Parliament.

The negotiation over terms of surrender for Oxford were protracted and dragged on for about a month. The House of Commons was still putting some pressure on Fairfax to use force rather than accept too generous a settlement and they rejected the first terms offered. They also seem to have held back from Fairfax and the Oxford garrison letters received from the king authorizing his governors to surrender. In the early days of June there was some rather half-hearted fighting, a party of cavalry charging out of the East Gate of the city and attempting unsuccessfuly to seize some cattle grazing outside the walls. They had more success with their artillery, which managed to return the fire aimed at them from Headington Hill and even caused some casualties within the camp there. Both sides had, however, agreed not to use the largest of their cannon. Outside Oxford, Shirburn surrendered, then Radcot and, on 12 June, Boarstall. It was agreed that Faringdon should be included in the same terms as were being discussed for Oxford, and so only Wallingford remained defiant in spite of being surrounded and its defences several times assaulted.

Fighting effectively stopped in Oxford on 17 June but there were still those in the city who objected to the proposed surrender, and the Lords of the Privy Council were afraid to meet in their usual place in Christ Church and went about armed with swords in case they were attacked in the streets by soldiers. Fairfax himself came into Oxford on 20 June and the surrender treaty was signed at Christ Church. That day the City Council, happy to see the end of its responsibility for the City Regiment, issued a testimonial to its commanding officer Lieutenant Colonel Francis Hall in exuberant language probably denoting their own feelings of joy and relief at the ending of the war as much as his deserts. They described him as 'vigilantly sedulous', 'actively valiant', 'courteously affable' and 'really just, soe farre as in him lay'. No servant of a council which had shown a marked reluctance to support the king's cause could have asked for more.

The date fixed officially for the final hand-over was 27 June, but, because the evacuation of the whole garrison could not be achieved in one day, the operation was carried out in stages. Prince Rupert and Prince Maurice were allowed to march out of the city with some ceremony, accompanied by three hundred 'gentlemen of quality'. They were to leave the country within ten days. On 24 June the main part of the garrison, about three thousand troops, marched out of the north and east gates of the city 'with the honours of war', flags flying and drums beating. They were given passes to travel home unmolested or to go to some convenient port within six months and to leave the country. The next day Fairfax brought in three regiments of his own troops to keep order in Oxford, and in particular he placed a guard around the Bodleian Library to preserve its books and manuscripts from the vandalism otherwise likely to be perpetrated by the extreme Puritan element in the Parliamentary army.

One other garrison, that of Wallingford commanded by the redoubtable Blagge, still held out for the king. The town was surrounded, but it had such good defences and in particular such a strong medieval castle, that it was proving impossible to capture. Unlike Banbury, where a similar problem had been overcome by offering the garrison generous terms to surrender, Blagge refused to treat. He had been refused permission to communicate with the king – a rather perverse refusal on the part of Parliament because it could well have led to an earlier surrender – and without Charles' express permission he would not consider negotiations. Fairfax was forced to bring up two extra regiments to attack Wallingford, and its proud commander was at last induced to seek terms. These were finally agreed when Blagge had received the king's order to surrender, on 27 July, a full month after Oxford. Like those of Banbury and Oxford, the surrender terms were generous. The garrison was allowed the privilege of marching out of the town with flags and drums, carrying their weapons.

CHAPTER 9

AFTER THE FIGHTING: WINNERS AND LOSERS

Without doubt the most common reaction to the end of the war was a sense of relief. There were of course those on the Royalist side like the garrison officers in Oxford, who resented surrender and would have fought on, or Colonel Blagge in Wallingford whose obstinate loyalty meant that he did fight on for another month, but for most ordinary people the cessation of hostilities was welcome. Bulstrode Whitelock described this widespread feeling (which he shared) among the people of Henley and the villages round about, when he invited them to come and 'slight' the wartime defences around Phyllis Court. He sought permission to demolish these ditches and earthworks as early as 6 May 1646, long before Oxford surrendered, which caused some surprise, but as he said himself 'he thirsted after the end of the war, and was the more desirous to have this garrison slighted because it was his own house'. He paid the soldiers of the garrison 6*d* a day above their wages and hired men from the surrounding villages, who came pouring in with mattocks, shovels and teams of horses to offer enthusiastic assistance. 'He threw down the breastworks and made handsome walkes of them on two sides, digged down the Bullworkes, sent away the great guns and ammunition and gott pay for his soldiers, whom he pleased, butt the countrey more, to see his readiness to slight garrisons.' One can still sense the joyful determination with which they worked to remove the hated evidence of war.

Peace would probably offer very different prospects to the various people involved in this happy scene. For the villagers it would indeed be a happy prospect, a return to the normal seasonal routines of country life free from the fear and privation they had experienced trying to survive in occupied territory close to a military garrison and

154

prey to passing armies seeking 'free quarter'. But for many life would not be quite as it had been before the war. Their resources were probably reduced already by wartime taxation, requisition and damage to crops. Husbands and sons who had gone off, or been 'pressed' to join one of those armies, were still away, and some would not return. The most their families would receive might be an account of death in some distant battle or siege brought back by a returning comrade. This would mean both a personal and an economic loss to the family now having to survive without them. Life was going to be hard for the next few years, but they expected it to be happy now that the war was ended. If they were Puritans they probably looked forward to a stricter moral tone in public and private life, and they might even have had hopes of social change bringing a more equal society. All the villagers would have had to find their own solution to the sensitive matter of living alongside former opponents, and some wounds would no doubt have been slow to heal. Historical documents do not tell us much about how people coped with these personal issues in the aftermath of war.

Whitelock says that he pleased the soldiers of the garrison by paying them 6*d* more than their normal daily wage. They were indeed lucky. Many soldiers would have been pleased to receive anything, as their pay was months in arrears, and this was to become a serious issue in the Parliamentary army in the next few years, regiments refusing to be disbanded before they were paid what was owing to them, and the question of pay arrears contributing to the the political discontent engendered by the Levellers. Ex-Royalist soldiers were even worse off as the penalty of being on the losing side was that they were disbanded on surrendering and were not in a position to bargain over arrears of pay. This explains the near mutiny of Blagge's Wallingford garrison when they suspected him of keeping for himself cash that could have been used to pay them. Soldiers from both sides who had been seriously wounded so that they could no longer work to support themselves and their families, were dependent on hand-outs from local poor rates, and there must have been many payments like that recorded in the Eynsham Churchwardens' accounts in 1649: 'Given to maimed soldiers . . . 6*d*'. Cromwell's New Model Army remained in being and had plenty of work in the next few years, creating for some a permanent career in the army – or in the navy, which was also strengthened under the Commonwealth – but for those who went back to civilian life there may have been difficult adjustments to make, as there are for soldiers after most wars.

As for Bulstrode Whitelock himself, he genuinely thirsted for peace, which was also in his case to bring considerable prosperity. His immediate concern was to set about repairing the loss and damage he had suffered to his properties in Henley. Fawley Court had been ransacked by Royalists early in the war and his other house at Phyllis Court, where he was now so energetically sweeping away the fortifications, had suffered almost as badly at the hands of his own side when it was converted to a fortress and occupied by an unruly garrison. Not far away was the ruin of another mansion, Greenland House belonging to the Royalist Sir John Doyley, which had been battered by heavy artillery and thoroughly looted by Browne's ill-disciplined soldiers in 1644. Doyley, like other Royalists, was heavily fined for his support of the king and was forced to sell what remained of Greenland – to Bulstrode Whitelock who added it to his extensive possessions in the Henley area. As a lawyer and diplomat held in high regard by Cromwell, Whitelock prospered and eventually became Ambassador to Sweden.

Another prominent lawyer from Oxfordshire, William Lenthall, had found himself at the forefront of public affairs both during and after the war by virtue of his position as Speaker of the House of Commons. He had grown wealthy through his legal practice and probably by exploiting his prominent position in Parliament. His house at Besselsleigh had been wrecked by soldiers from Abingdon who were intent on rendering it useless to the Royalists as a garrison, but he also owned Burford Priory which remained intact. Surprisingly, he later fell out with Cromwell and deserted his former colleagues, seeking to save his own neck at the Restoration. Having retired to Burford Priory, he eventually died in 1662 and was buried in Burford parish church, but perhaps with a pang of conscience for his behaviour, stipulated in his will that he should have only a plain memorial with the inscription 'Vermis Sum'. His famous defence of the rights of the Commons against Charles I is much better remembered today than the circumstances of his later life.

For those not involved at such a high level the resumption of local politics and administration quickly occupied their minds. In Oxford the City Council wasted no time at all in repealing the resolution, passed under pressure from the king, debarring certain 'disaffected persons' who were known Parliamentary sympathizers from holding office. They then proceeded to the election of a new mayor, and chose John Nixon, perhaps the most disaffected of them all. Their position as supporters of the new regime was obvious for all to see. The position of the university was more uncertain and it now had to use all its experience and influence to preserve its privileges. With the university in trouble for supporting the king, the City Council hoped to redress the balance in the age-old town and gown dispute but they were upstaged once again by the university, so that little progress was made. However, in the immediate aftermath of war Puritan preachers were appointed to weed out the most outspoken Royalists and High Churchmen in the colleges, and Anthony Wood was typically scathing in his descriptions of them: 'Cornish and Langley, two fooles; Reynolds and Harrys, two knaves; Cheynell and rabbi Wilkinson, two madmen'. When in 1648 Wood had to appear before the 'Visitors' appointed by Parliament to declare that he accepted their authority he prevaricated, pretending not to understand the question, and he only avoided being evicted from the college because his mother used her influence to protect him, 'otherwise,' as he said himself, 'he had infallibly gon to the pot'.

Political and religious wrangling between the many different factions in the county was to go on for years, but the immediate task at the end of the war was simply to pick up the pieces, repair the damage and try to get back to a normal routine of daily life. Damage was considerable in towns like Oxford, Banbury, Wallingford and Faringdon, which had been subjected to siege or direct attack. In Oxford the houses of people living in suburbs outside the defences like Wolvercote, Hinksey and St Clements had been purposely demolished by the defenders, while the great fire of October 1644 had destroyed many more on the west side of the city – as much as a quarter of the houses in the town by one estimate.

Banbury by all accounts was even worse, having suffered two long sieges. Few houses or other buildings could have escaped some

(1)

To the Supream Authority of the
Nation, the Commons in Parliament affembled.

The humble Reprefentation and Petition
of divers wel-affected Gentlemen, Free-
houlders, and others of the County of
Oxon.

Humbly sheweth,

Hat our Spirits are much revived, and
our hearts raifed up in the fenfible
apprehenfion of the good hand of
God upon you, in your late and pre-
fent actings, in referrence to Common Right and freedom, and for as
much as your work tends to the wel-being of this

A 2   Com-

A petition of 1649 from the Gentlemen of Oxfordshire
addressed 'To the Supream Authority of the Nation, the
Commons in Parliament assembled.'

damage either from the bombardment of the castle or the fighting that took place in the streets, or just the wanton damage that happens when armies fight over possession of a town or occupy it for a long time. The Cavaliers from the castle were said to have set many houses on fire on one occasion out of revenge for the hostility of the Puritan townsfolk. The Council ceased to function some time in 1645 and much of the population who could find somewhere else to go had fled. When the castle finally surrendered in 1646 Banbury presented a very sorry sight: Joshua Sprigge graphically described it as having been 'once a greate and faire market town before the late troubles, but now having scarce the one halfe standing to gaze on the ruines of the other'. It fell to the Council to organize the repair of public buildings, but first of all they had to petition Parliament to legitimize the position of Aholiab West as mayor. He had been elected in September 1644, but when his year of office officially ended in 1645 it had not been possible to elect a sucessor because 'the Town and Borough of Banbury and castle there were so infested with bloody and cruel enemies, who burnt and pulled down a great part of the said town, that the Mayor and most of the Aldermen and Burgesses, by reason of their cruelty, were constrained to fly out of the said Town and Borough to save their Lives'. It was agreed that Aholiab West should continue as mayor for another year. A month later Parliament (which not surprisingly showed a good deal of sympathy for Banbury's sufferings) also agreed to a request from the inhabitants of Banbury that they should be allowed to have the timber and boards cut down in Forrest Wood near Oxford and sequestered from one Mr Powell, 'a Malignant', to be used 'for the repair of the Church and Steeple, and rebuilding of the Vicarage House and Common Gaol there'. Any timber left over from this work was to be disposed of by the local MPs to 'well affected persons' of the town for rebuilding their houses.

The cutting down of woods and standing trees in parks belonging to 'malignants' (anyone supporting the other side) was another kind of destruction common throughout Oxfordshire. Both armies had need of wood for repairing carts and waggons, making temporary shelters, for fuel and for dozens of other uses, while large quantities were needed in occupied towns for defensive works. Cutting down standing timber belonging to an enemy was a form of punishment whose effect would be felt for years afterwards. Dr Plot, writing his *Natural History of Oxfordshire* in the 1670s commented that whereas timber had been a plentiful commodity in the county before the war, it became so scarce afterwards that it was sold by weight at a high price 'everywhere but in the Chiltern country' where it was still more readily available.

Apart from such supplies of timber from elsewhere, the town of Banbury was largely rebuilt out of the ruins of the castle. Nothing could be more appropriate to the inhabitants who had suffered so much, than that the hated Royalist stronghold which had been at the centre of their troubles should be pulled down, and the materials used to rebuild their ruined homes. The only problem was that the hated Royalist stronghold had been seized from the Puritan Lord Saye and Sele, and was rightly part of his family's inheritance. In the end a financial deal was struck, under the terms of which Lord Saye was to receive £8,000 in compensation (raised by sequestering Royalist estates in Oxfordshire, Northamptonshire and Warwickshire), and the castle was to be demolished and the materials given to the people of the town. The work was mainly carried out in 1648 and was no doubt approached with great enthusiasm by the inhabitants. Archaeologists trying to reconstruct the plan of the castle in the 1970s noted that only robbed-out foundation trenches remained to show the position of the curtain wall and outer gate, all usable stone having been dug out of them even below ground level. They found plenty of seventeenth-century rubbish, lead musket balls and parts of a cannon.

The other castles which had been used as Royalist strongholds were similarly 'slighted', Oxford's being demolished in 1651 and Wallingford's a year later. Some parts of Oxford castle were left standing, however, including St George's tower and the Court House, and the castle mound which can still be seen today.

Many churches throughout the county had suffered damage either in the course of the fighting or through the action of Puritan iconoclasts. Banbury parish church was so badly damaged that in spite of repairs it was eventually pulled down and replaced in the eighteenth century, Faringdon lost its spire and Radley one side of its nave. St Leonard's, Wallingford, had the apse and south aisle destroyed. Internal damage was frequently caused by zealous Puritan soldiers who went about destroying anything considered 'Popish'. This

An attractive public garden now adorns the site of Wallingford's castle, the
scene of much fierce fighting and the last Royalist stronghold to surrender.

usually meant statues of the Virgin and saints, stained-glass windows
and altar rails. The statue of the Virgin and Child over the door of St
Mary the Virgin Church in High Street, Oxford, was one of the first
casualties, being shot at by Parliamentary troops as they were leaving
the city in September 1642 before the battle of Edgehill. There are
empty niches in the nave of Chipping Norton church and traditions
passed down for generations in many Oxfordshire parishes attribute
serious damage to Puritan soldiers though few of these incidents can
now be proved. It was certainly common practice during the war to
make use of church buildings as temporary accommodation for
soldiers or stabling for horses, and they were also convenient prisons
on some occasions. These uses undoubtedly led to damage to the
interior. The famous Jesse window in Dorchester Abbey still bears
witness to this in the mutilated figure of the Virgin which surmounts
it, and as organs were another target of Puritan disapproval, Thame
lost its new organ when the soldiers dismantled it and 'went tooting
about the town' with its pipes. The tomb of Lord Williams was also
damaged by soldiers lighting fires on it to cook their food, and the

A contemporary picture of Puritan soldiers destroying
altar rails and other objectionable features in a church.

tomb of Sir John Walter at Wolvercote is just one example of
memorials to prominent Royalist families being attacked. The king
himself was responsible for requisitioning the bells of Deddington
church and melting them down for armaments. The tower of the
church had collapsed before the war and there was an inevitable delay
in rebuilding it. Charles did promise to repay the value of the bells
after the war.

A shining example of a Parliamentarian soldier who had the
courage to stand up against the zealots and protect his local church
was Francis Martyn of Ewelme. Tradition says that he stood with his
back to the door of the church, sword in hand, and prevented the
destruction of the wonderful medieval decoration and the tomb of
Alice Chaucer. He rightly has his own memorial in this church.
Cleaning out the mess left by soldiers and their horses was a frequent
charge on the churchwardens' accounts at Abingdon, and more
expensive damage was caused to the interior of Woodstock church by
Royalist prisoners taken at Colchester in the second brief outbreak of
war in 1648. They were being moved from Colchester to the port of
Bristol prior to being transported to the West Indies and were lodged
in the church at Woodstock for several weeks, where they broke up the
wooden pews 'except two or three which the mayor and aldermen
used to sit in' and burnt them in order to keep warm in their

otherwise unheated prison. (William Lenthall, who was MP for Woodstock, offered his fees as Recorder of the Borough to pay for the repairs.) Apart from churches themselves, the market crosses at Abingdon and Burford were both demolished on the orders of Waller, because he considered them superstitious relics, and the cornmarket building in the centre of Oxford was stripped of its lead roof in order to make Royalist bullets.

There were obviously economic losses for many individuals, cottagers and small farmers who were invaded by passing armies demanding lodging and food, pilfering anything that took their fancy and damaging standing crops or driving off livestock. The official requisitioning of horses and carts was a very serious loss to a farmer whose livelihood depended on such irreplaceable equipment. If they were properly hired and paid for the loss might only amount to a temporary inconvenience, but if they were seized and not returned, or destroyed in a skirmish, it could cause real hardship. Anyone liable to taxation suffered particularly from the very large amounts levied to

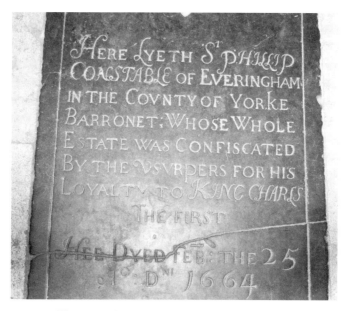

The memorial to a disgruntled Royalist in Steeple
Barton church.

pay for the war and in parts of Oxfordshire this meant paying taxes to both sides. Royalist landowners who had their estates sequestered by Parliament could only recover them through paying very heavy fines. Landlords found it increasingly difficult to collect their rents so that income from normal sources fell just when demands on them were increasing. Anthony Wood had to leave school in Thame in 1646 because his mother could no longer afford to keep him there 'she having suffered much in her estate by the late dreadful fire in Oxon.' Known Parliamentary sympathizers living in occupied Oxfordshire during the war were punished by aggressive and expensive billeting and even by imprisonment and ransom. They could at least seek compensation from Parliament after the war as did William Diston of Chipping Norton, whose petition in 1655 referred to 'his sufferings and losses for the State, he having been several times taken prisoner and forced to pay large sums for his redemption'. He also speaks of 'frequent plunderings'. He had to borrow £600 in order to ransom his elderly uncle Henry Cornish, who had also been carried off to Oxford Castle. He was awarded £250 – only a small part of his losses. Michael Molyns of Wallingford must have been unusual in obtaining compensation from both sides. He apparently received £66 12s 3d out of the sale of materials from the castle when it was demolished, but after the Restoration received a much larger sum from Charles II's parliament in recompense for the burning of his house during the war.

High Church clergy were natural targets for the Puritan regime after the war and were liable to be evicted from their parishes. Unless they had other sources of income or friends who would help them, this might reduce them to an unaccustomed state of poverty. The churchwardens of Eynsham in 1649 paid out 2s 'to a poore Minister his wife and children', and later 6d to 'another Minister'. Perhaps these were evicted Anglicans. Thomas Wyatt survived at Ducklington in spite of his Royalist sympathies, perhaps because they were not too outspoken. He continued as rector until his death in 1667. Others were less fortunate: the Revd George Morecroft of Kingham was removed and replaced by a Puritan called Thomas Jackson. Morecroft, however, although seventy-two years old refused to go quietly and made two attempts to repossess the rectory, on the second occasion bringing with him a band of supporters who used 'force and violence' against Jackson. Morecroft's final removal was only achieved after an appeal to Lord Saye and Sele and an order from the House of Lords.

Not everyone was a loser by the war. As in any war there were opportunities for profit and men ready to take advantage of them. The presence of the court and army in Oxford meant not only overcrowding and shortages, but a greatly increased market for all kinds of goods often at inflated prices because of the shortages. Some tradesmen must have done very well during the war years although in dealing with a shifting population of soldiers they ran the risk of unpaid bills. Outside Oxford too, although local markets were disrupted by the difficulty and danger of moving produce along the country roads, there were more mouths to feed and some of the time at least the goods would be legitimately bought. Craftsmen whose skills were in demand, such as blacksmiths, farriers and wheelwrights must have done particularly well, as did the tailors who were needed to supply the army with clothes. Although the rolls of cloth might be seized from Wiltshire clothiers, local men were needed to turn it into uniforms, and the resident tailors of Oxford, normally protected by their guild restrictions, complained bitterly that 'foreign' tailors were being allowed to practise their trade within the city. The accounts of the Royalist Ordnance in Oxford give clear evidence of payments to other tradesmen:

> You are out of such money as now remayneth in your Custody to pay to ye bearers hereof, Thomas Finch, Thomas Horneley and William Careless, the some of ten pound to be distributed amongst fifty Carters that brought five and twenty loads of Iron and round shot of Iron from his Majesty's garrison at Evesham to the Citty of Oxon . . .
>
> > Rich. March to Lord Percy, General
> > of HM Trayne of Artillery

> I have likewise treated with a ploumber here whoe will undertake the makinge of one tonne of muskett shott weeklye after the rate of £16 per tonne, upon weekelye payments.

There were also those who prospered in less legitimate ways from the chaos which inevitably followed the ending of four years of civil war. The Eynsham churchwardens' accounts again include a sequence of payments which tell their own story:

For a key to the church porch dore	£0 0s 6d
for mending the tower door lock	£0 0s 8d
for the glaisier mending the church windows	£0 6s 0d
for sending hues and cries for the church goods lost	£0 0s 8d

Perhaps this was the work of some small-time thief or unpaid soldier, but crime on a much bigger scale was the career adopted by some disbanded Cavaliers, unwilling to return to a quiet civilian life after the excitements and bravado of serving in one of the king's cavalry regiments and now disgraced and bitter in defeat. In the years after the war the roads around London and in some other parts became unsafe for travellers because of the presence of these 'highwaymen' as they came to be called, but the most notorious of them all, (and the archetype of all highwaymen long before the days of Dick Turpin) was the self-styled 'Captain' James Hind, born the son of a respectable saddler in Chipping Norton. After an apprenticeship with a gang of thieves in London before the war, he joined the Royalist army no doubt tempted by the promise of adventure and the scope for legitimized robbery. He was a member of Compton's Horse and may have been among the defenders of Banbury Castle. After the war he took to the road and became the subject of ballads and legends. He earned a romantic popular image by his wit and gallantry towards ladies and his reputation for being generous to the poor. One typical story recounts that he was forced by his own needs to take money from a poor farmer on his way back from Wantage market but kept his promise to repay the man with interest a week later. As an ex-Cavalier he seems to have specialized in robbing Parliamentarians, and is claimed to have once tried to hold up the Lord Protector's coach. In spite of all the myths that surround Hind and his like, they were a menace to innocent travellers and demonstrated the temporary breakdown of law and order in the period immediately following the war. Hind rejoined the army to fight for Charles II at the Battle of

Worcester, but was captured soon afterwards, and it was in that city that he was hanged, drawn and quartered in 1652. Anthony Wood heard of Hind's exploits, describing him as 'a little dapper desperat fellow' and also wrote about another Oxfordshire thief called Haywood who was captured and imprisoned in Oxford castle, 'but soon after, endeavouring to make an escape by the help of his sheets and bedcords tyed together to let him down from a high place, brake his legg and was taken'.

Gangs of former soldiers turned highway robbers were operating on the roads of Oxfordshire at this time, and the High Sherrif had to call out a posse comitatus of local men to round up about one hundred of them described as 'Troopers, Irish and others who had been in arms against the Parlement' early in 1647.

Even those soldiers in the pay of Parliament could still cause problems through their behaviour towards civilians. Whitelock learned in June 1647 of the death of his sister, the wife of Sir James Dixon of Little Rollright, which he attributed to her treatment by soldiers billeted in her house: 'A troupe of the Parlement's quartered at her house in her husband's absence, she then lying in having been brought to bed about 14 dayes before. Yett the barbarous domineering soldiers would not admit this for an excuse, nor be content with their quarters, though fit for better men, but compelled her (though in that condition) to rise out of her bed to make better preparations for them, with which she took cold, fell into a feaver and dyed.'

Bulstrode Whitelock was a member of the committee appointed by the House of Commons to consider a 'Humble Representation and Petition of divers well-affected Gentlemen, Freeholders and others of the County of Oxon' presented to them in April 1649. It called for more progress in sweeping away the vestiges of Royalist influence in the county and in the university, and measures to ensure that only 'the well-affected of this County, who have been always faithful to your proceedings (and none else)' should be able to vote for the county's MPs or stand for election. It was addressed to 'The Supream Authority of the Nation, the Commons in Parliament assembled', because it was written three months after the execution of the king.

The single blow of the axe which beheaded King Charles I in January 1649 was perhaps as significant as all the blows and shots that had been delivered in winning the war. Execution of the king had not of course been Parliament's aim at the outset of war; it had become the only way forward for Cromwell only since the repeated failure of attempts to reach a negotiated settlement. It opened up the huge and intriguing debate about what sort of government the country was to have in future. That debate had already been going on, but it now took a huge leap forward. The act of execution itself, and some of the democratic possibilities it opened up, also lost Cromwell many of his former supporters on the conservative wing of Parliament. Notwithstanding their opposition to the Divine Right theory as practised by Charles, some of them probably still harboured a lingering belief in the sacred nature of the Crown as an institution, so that they could not see the execution of the king simply as a practical and necessary expedient. Furthermore, there was a widespread feeling among the nobility and gentry that the whole order of society was threatened and the way opened to all kinds of extreme democratic ideas, which would sweep away their recognized position as leaders. Such fears were well founded. The abolition of the House of Lords (which was achieved) and the proposal of the Levellers to give more people the right to vote (which was not), frightened even such staunch opponents of the king as Lord Saye and Sele, who objected to the idea of 'sitting alongside brewers and draymen' and took himself off to live on Lundy Island in the Bristol Channel for the duration of the Commonwealth. (Because he thus distanced himself from the Commonwealth, he was able to survive the Restoration unscathed, and was appointed Lord Privy Seal under Charles II.) Similarly, the Earl of Essex was clearly no republican and had asked even before the end of the war: 'Is this the liberty which we claim to vindicate by shedding our blood? Posterity will say that to deliver them from the yoke of the king we have subjugated them to that of the common people.' Liberty and democracy had different shades of meaning for different groups of people; for most they seemed to mean greater power for their particular section of society.

The Commons itself was divided between a mainly Presbyterian group of MPs who wanted to impose their own style of church on the nation and keep political power in the hands of their own class, and more liberal-minded men like Henry Martin of Hinton Manor in

Oxfordshire (though MP for Buckinghamshire) who were much more sympathetic to the new ideas about liberty and democracy.

Groups such as the Levellers voiced arguments for greater democracy well in advance of most other people of their time. They held that ultimate power in the state lay with the people themselves and they put forward demands which included votes for all 'free' men, shorter parliaments and more frequent elections (giving greater control over MPs), a form of proportional representation, paid MPs (so that not only the wealthy could stand), religious toleration, and equality of all before the law. In general terms they sought an end to privilege and a much more equal sharing of political power among the people of England, although by no means everyone would have had the right to vote. They did not go as far as other communistic groups like the 'Diggers' who sought to return all land to common ownership, taking it out of private hands. Much of what the Levellers argued for seems acceptable today, but to the Presbyterian party in Parliament in the 1640s and to some extent to Cromwell himself, they appeared far too revolutionary. Cromwell, who was sympathetic to some degree of greater democracy, found himself between the opposing extremes of conservative and radical groups. The army was another factor in the political debate, and its concerns over arrears of pay and indemnity for actions committed in the war were exploited by the Levellers so that they eventually led to a mutiny by several regiments in the spring of 1649. Representatives of the common soldiers in all the regiments had been elected to debate the army's grievances with the officers and with Cromwell, Fairfax and Ireton, and the Levellers had introduced their political programme into the debate in a historic document called *The Agreement of the People*. However, by early 1649 they felt that they were getting nowhere, their leaders had been imprisoned and the final straw was Cromwell's decision to send part of the army to Ireland (including the 'Leveller' regiments) to campaign against the Catholics. Apart from finding this distasteful to their ideas on liberty, they saw it as a way of removing them from the political debate in England.

The final showdown between Cromwell and the Levellers happened in Oxfordshire in May 1649. There were mutinies in several army regiments, mainly in Salisbury but also in Banbury where Captain

William Thompson supported by about two hundred other soldiers published a pamphlet complaining about the suppression of freedom by Parliament, Cromwell and the army officers. Parliament's reaction was to take precautions for the security of London and to send Colonel Reynolds to attack the mutineers. There was some fighting at Warkworth to the east of Banbury and although other Levellers came from Oxford to join him, Thompson's forces were dispersed, he himself together with some of his men escaping in the direction of Chipping Norton. At the same time the much larger number of Levellers from the regiments which had mutinied in Salisbury set off to join up with their colleagues at Banbury.

Fairfax and Cromwell could not afford to see their army weakened by mutiny and decided on swift action to put down the mutineers and finally silence the Levellers' dangerous cry for democracy. With great speed they marched loyal troops after them and when they were near Wantage sent officers to make offers of talks before any attempt was made to use force. This may well have lulled the Levellers into a false sense of safety. Even when they found their crossing of the Thames blocked by soldiers at Newbridge, they made no attempt to fight, instead accepting the help of the local people to get across at Duxford. They had gathered more support from other regiments in the area and on Sunday 13 May proceeded as far as Burford and lodged there for the night. Just a few hours later, as they were settling into their quarters, they were completely surprised and overwhelmed by Fairfax's troops bursting in on them from one side of the town, while Cromwell's attacked simultaneously from the other. They were outnumbered, caught off guard and unable to offer any resistance, and in any case had perhaps expected to discuss their grievances rather than be attacked and rounded up as prisoners. About 340 were captured, disarmed and driven into the church, where they were locked up. The parish church became their prison for the next three days and nights.

They were anxious days and long nights. Worse than the physical discomfort to which all Civil War soldiers were hardened, was the uncertainty about their punishment. All the excitement of the stand they had made in Salisbury for their ideals of freedom and democracy, the exhilaration of their triumphant march and the comradeship they had felt towards each other and the recruits who had joined them, had quickly melted away in the disaster of their sudden defeat. They were harangued by Cromwell himself, and between the bouts of despondent or defiant talk in the church, one of them whiled away the long hours by scratching his name, Anthony Sedley, in the lead of the font, and underneath it wrote '1649, prisner'. We know nothing else about this soldier, but his name is preserved over three centuries later.

Cromwell's final judgement was typical of his method of dealing with looters and other criminals in the army during the war, for he clearly wished the Levellers to be seen as mutineers and not as heroes of democracy. Three ringleaders, Cornet Thompson (brother of the Banbury leader), Corporal Perkins and Private Church were singled out for execution. A fourth, called Denne, was also condemned but cried and pleaded so convincingly that he was pardoned – giving rise to lasting suspicions that he was Cromwell's agent. As the rest of the prisoners were made to climb onto the leads of the church roof to watch, the three victims were brought out of the church, blinking in the sunlight of a bright May morning. The churchyard was filled with soldiers of the loyal regiments, and no doubt the people of the town who had gathered to see the end of this unexpected episode. The

The Levellers' memorial on the wall of Burford church,
where they were shot for mutiny and attempting to
achieve a greater degree of democracy than Cromwell
was prepared to countenance.

small contingent selected to form the firing-squad faced them as the three were lined up against the church wall; an order was given, shots echoed around the churchyard, and the limits of democracy under Cromwell were firmly established.

A few days later, after the soldiers and their prisoners had marched away, the churchwardens made a payment to 'Daniel Munke and others for cleaning the church when the Levellers were taken . . . 3*s* 6*d*', and later still the vicar recorded the three deaths in his burial register without any details. Cromwell and Fairfax, on their way back to London, paused in Oxford where the university entertained them to dinner to celebrate their success.

This was effectively the end of the Leveller movement, although later the same year soldiers in Oxford made a further stand which was quickly put down. Two more Levellers were shot near Gloucester Green, Privates Biggs and Piggen. It was also the final chapter of the Civil War as far as Oxfordshire was concerned, which like other counties now had to come to terms with the Commonwealth, and in time would apparently welcome back with open arms the restored monarchy of Charles II. It would be a very long time before such freedom as the Levellers had dared to dream of would be achieved.

APPENDIX

Burials Recorded in Some Local Parishes 1636–46

	1636	1637	1638	1639	1640	1641	1642	1643	1644	1645	1646
Adderbury	33	19	27	37	15	38	25	20	26	26	19
Bicester	34	18	23	21	29	19	18	62	37	42	21
Bradwell	5	6	15	6	3	9	16	10	12	10	28
Burford	40	42	45	56	44	37	48	89	69	42	41
Caversham	16	14	12	16	14	5	1	43	21	12	10
Cropredy	8	6	27	21	8	26	19	16	20	12	13
Ducklington	4	10	3	8	10	9	1	12	11	10	6
Horsepath	1	1	1	1	2	6	3	12	19	2	3
Standlake	12	12	6	26	8	4	6	24	11	20	7
Swalcliffe	19	12	7	9	9	13	19	20	20	9	9
Thame	39	26	34	40	41	53	47	189	45	23	30
Wantage	77	36	47	52	32	68	55	52	94	51	54
Witney	62	49	56	48	61	75	91	157	102	79	47

Registers for the following places are incomplete

	1636	1637	1638	1639	1640	1641	1642	1643	1644	1645	1646
Oxford*	179	113	125	168	167	235	161	841	437	292	193
Banbury	73	119	85	99	79	98	51	253	293	211	31**
Henley	68	57	56	106	67	84	58	229	70		

* excluding the parishes of St Thomas, St Aldate and St Clement
** part of the year only

Registers for many parishes are incomplete or have not survived at all from this period. The burials shown in the above tables are the total number recorded for the places named, of which very few are identified as soldiers. The pattern clearly shows a marked increase in civilian deaths during the war, especially in the year 1643. It is most likely that this was due to the spread of plague and other diseases, made much worse than usual by the presence of the soldiers.

SOURCES

Abbreviations: COS, Centre for Oxfordshire Studies; OxonArch, Oxfordshire County Archives; OxArch, Oxford City Archives; Bod, Bodleian Library. The sources are given in the order to which they refer in each chapter.

Introduction

Mercurius Publicus, 10–17 May 1660, COS
F. Thompson, *Lark Rise to Candleford*, 1939

Chapter 1

I.G. Phillip, 'River Navigation at Oxford During the Civil War and Common-wealth', in *Oxoniensia*, vol. I, 1937
R. Spalding (ed.), *The Diary of Bulstrode Whitelock*, 1990
Journal of Thomas Wyatt, Rector of Ducklington, Bod, MS top Oxon C378
'King Charles I's Visit to Oxford', contemporary letter, in *Oxoniensia*, vol. I, 1936
M. Cox, *History of Abingdon*, vol. III, 1993
Victoria County History of Oxfordshire
F. Emery, *The Oxfordshire Landscape*, 1974
E. Marshall, *Early History of Woodstock Manor*, 1873
J. Washbourn (ed.), Sgt. Henry Foster's Account of the Earl of Essex's march, in *Bibliotheca Gloucestrensis*, 1825
E.R.C. Brinkworth (ed.), *South Newington Churchwardens Accounts 1553–1684*, Banbury Historical Society, 1964 (Originals in OxonArch)

Chapter 2

A. Beesley, *History of Banbury*, 1841
E. Meades, *History of Chipping Norton*, 1984

C.S.A. Dobson (ed.), *Oxfordshire Protestation Returns*, Ox. Record Society, 1955
Cox, op.cit.
Victoria County History of Oxfordshire
Cavalier Songs and Ballads of England, Mackay, Griffin, Bohn & Co., 1863
Wyatt, op.cit.
H.E. Salter (ed.), Oxford City Council Acts
Anthony Wood, *Athenae Oxoniensis*, 1691
A. Clark (ed.), *The Life and Times of Anthony Wood*, vol. I, 1892
Churchwardens' accounts for Oddington, Langford and Pyrton, OxonArch
C.H. Firth, 'Chronological Summary of the Civil War in Oxfordshire, Buckinghamshire and Berkshire', in *Proceedings of the Oxford Architectural and Historical Society*, 1890
A. Carter and J. Stevenson, *The Oxfordshire Area in the Civil War*, Radio Oxford, 1974

Chapter 3

Spalding, op.cit.
Victoria County History of Oxfordshire
A. Ballard, *Chronicles of the Royal Borough of Woodstock*, 1896
Beesley, op.cit.
Wyatt, op.cit.
Wood, op.cit.
P. Tennant, *Edgehill and Beyond*, 1992

Chapter 4

Wood, op.cit.
I. Roy (ed.), Royalist Ordinance Papers,

174

Oxford Record Society, vol. XLIII 1965

Journal of Sir Samuel Luke, Bod MS. Eng.Hist. c. 53 (Transcript ed. I.G. Phillip, Oxford Record Society, 1947)

Clarendon, Earl of, History of the Great Rebellion, ed. W.D. Macray, 1888

Letters held by Exeter College

Oxford City Council Minutes, Act Books, Audit Volumes and Civil War Charities Volume, OxArch

Registers of Oxford parishes in OxonArch

Chapter 5

The Desires of the Commissioners for the Weekly Loan to His Majesty's Horse, pamphlet, COS

Burial registers of many Oxfordshire parishes, originals in OxonArch and transcripts also in COS. Those for Banbury have been published by Banbury Historical Society. Churchwardens' accounts are also held in OxonArch

Cox, op.cit.

Wood, op.cit.

Tennant, op.cit.

Spalding, op.cit.

Wyatt Journal, op.cit.

C. Sherwood, *Civil War in the Midlands*, 1992

C. Carlton, *Going to the Wars, The Impact of the British Civil Wars 1638–51*, 1992

P. Slack, *The Impact of Plague in Tudor and Stuart England*, 1985

N. Cooper, *Aynho, a Northamptonshire Village*, 1984

Luke Journal, op.cit.

A True Relation of the Taking of Cirencester, pamphlet, COS

Chapter 6

Mercurius Aulicus, COS

J. Stevenson and A. Carter, 'The Raid on Chinnor and the Fight at Chalgrove Field', in *Oxoniensia*, 1972

Luke Journal, op.cit.

Beesley, op.cit.

Foster Account, op.cit.

Chapter 7

Cox, op.cit.

Luke Journal, op.cit.

Revd V. Thomas, *Account of the Night March of King Charles I*, 1850, COS

P. Young and M.Toynbee, *Cropredy Bridge*, 1970

Tennant, op.cit.

Beesley, op.cit. (inc. quotations from *The Moderate Intelligencer* and *The Perfect Dimnal*. Originals of such news-sheets can be found among the *Thomason Tracts*: the British Library.)

Chapter 8

Cox, op.cit.

Tennant, op.cit.

Wood, op.cit.

Beesley, op.cit.

Mercurius Aulicus, COS

Marshall, op.cit.

F.J. Varley, *The Siege of Oxford*, 1932

Sites and Monuments Record (Abingdon burials), COS

Chapter 9

Wood, op.cit.

Spalding, op.cit.

Beesley, op.cit.

R. Plot, *The Natural History of Oxfordshire*, 1677

Dictionary of National Biography

K. Rodwell, 'Excavations at Banbury Castle', in *Cake and Cockhorse*, vol. V, 1974

S. Spencer Pearce, 'The Parish Church of Woodstock and an Episode in the Civil War', in *Transactions of Oxfordshire Archaeological Society*, 1929

R. Mann, *The Rectors of Kingham*, 1990

Roy, op.cit.

O.M. Meades, *The Adventures of Captain James Hind*, 1985

Petition of Divers Well Affected Gentlemen, pamphlet, COS

INDEX